First World War
and Army of Occupation
War Diary
France, Belgium and Germany

39 DIVISION
117 Infantry Brigade
Sherwood Foresters
(Nottinghamshire and Derbyshire Regiment)
16th Battalion
6 March 1916 - 22 May 1919

WO95/2587/1

The Naval & Military Press Ltd
www.nmarchive.com
Published in association with The National Archives

Published by

The Naval & Military Press Ltd

Unit 10 Ridgewood Industrial Park,

Uckfield, East Sussex,

TN22 5QE England

Tel: +44 (0) 1825 749494

www.naval-military-press.com

www.nmarchive.com

This diary has been reprinted in facsimile from the original. Any imperfections are inevitably reproduced and the quality may fall short of modern type and cartographic standards.

© **Crown Copyright**
Images reproduced by permission of The National Archives, London, England, 2015.

Contents

Document type	Place/Title	Date From	Date To
Heading	WO95/2587/1		
Heading	117th Brigade. 39th Division. (Chatsworth Rifles) Battalion disembarked Havre 7.3.16 1/16th Battalion Notts & Derby Regiment March 1916		
War Diary	Witley Camp	06/03/1916	06/03/1916
War Diary	Havre	07/03/1916	08/03/1916
War Diary	Steenbecque	09/03/1916	13/03/1916
War Diary	Dump House Sailly	14/03/1916	18/03/1916
War Diary	Estaires	19/03/1916	28/03/1916
War Diary	Bethune	29/03/1916	29/03/1916
War Diary	Annequin South	29/03/1916	30/03/1916
Heading	117th Brigade. 39th Division 1/16th Battalion Notts & Derby Regiment April 1916		
War Diary	Auchy	01/04/1916	05/04/1916
War Diary	Busnettes	06/04/1916	16/04/1916
War Diary	Riez Du Vinage	17/04/1916	22/04/1916
War Diary	Festubert	23/04/1916	27/04/1916
War Diary	Rue De Lepinette	28/04/1916	30/04/1916
Heading	117th Brigade. 39th Division. 1/16th Battalion Notts & Derby Regiment May 1916		
War Diary	Rue De Lepinette	01/05/1916	01/05/1916
War Diary	Festubert	02/05/1916	05/05/1916
War Diary	Le Touret	06/05/1916	09/05/1916
War Diary	Riez Du Vinage	10/05/1916	16/05/1916
War Diary	Givenchy	17/05/1916	29/05/1916
War Diary	Gorre	30/05/1916	31/05/1916
Heading	117th Brigade. 39th Division. 1/16th Battalion Notts & Derby Regiment June 1916		
War Diary	Gorre	03/06/1916	03/06/1916
War Diary	Givenchy	03/06/1916	06/06/1916
War Diary	Essars	06/06/1916	07/06/1916
War Diary	Les Chocquaux	08/06/1916	10/06/1916
War Diary	Le Touret	11/06/1916	16/06/1916
War Diary	Ferme Du Bois	17/06/1916	30/06/1916
Heading	117th Brigade. 39th Division. 1/16th Battalion Notts & Derby Regiment July 1916		
War Diary	Ferme Du Bois	01/07/1916	20/07/1916
War Diary	Canal House Gorre	21/07/1916	23/07/1916
War Diary	Bethune	24/07/1916	24/07/1916
War Diary	Tuning Fork.	26/07/1916	31/07/1916
Heading	117th Brigade. 39th Division. 1/16th Battalion Notts & Derby Regiment August 1916		
War Diary	Gorre.	01/08/1916	01/08/1916
War Diary	Givenchy	02/08/1916	06/08/1916
War Diary	Le Hamel	07/08/1916	09/08/1916
War Diary	Bethune	10/08/1916	10/08/1916
War Diary	Auchel	11/08/1916	11/08/1916
War Diary	La Thieuloye	14/08/1916	23/08/1916
War Diary	Buneville	24/08/1916	24/08/1916
War Diary	Neuvellette	25/08/1916	25/08/1916

War Diary	Auchie	26/08/1916	28/08/1916
Heading	117th Brigade. 39th Division. 1/16th Battalion Notts & Derby Regiment September 1916		
War Diary	Beaussart.	01/09/1916	02/09/1916
War Diary	Beaumont Hamel.	03/09/1916	14/09/1916
War Diary	Mailly Wood	16/09/1916	20/09/1916
War Diary	Hebuterne	21/09/1916	30/09/1916
Heading	117th Brigade. 39th Division. 1/16th Battalion Notts & Derby Regiment October 1916		
War Diary	Hebuterne	01/10/1916	01/10/1916
War Diary	Bertrancourt	03/10/1916	03/10/1916
War Diary	Martinsart Wood	05/10/1916	05/10/1916
War Diary	Thiepval	06/10/1916	10/10/1916
War Diary	Senlis	11/10/1916	16/10/1916
War Diary	Thiepval	17/10/1916	17/10/1916
War Diary	River Ancre Sector	18/10/1916	26/10/1916
War Diary	Pioneer Road.	26/10/1916	26/10/1916
War Diary	Thiepval	27/10/1916	28/10/1916
War Diary	Martinsart Wood	29/10/1916	31/10/1916
Heading	117th Brigade. 39th Division. 1/16th Battalion Notts & Derby Regiment November 1916		
War Diary	Martinsart Wood	02/11/1916	02/11/1916
War Diary	Paisley Dump.	03/11/1916	05/11/1916
War Diary	Senlis	06/11/1916	06/11/1916
War Diary	Paisley Dump	07/11/1916	07/11/1916
War Diary	South Bluff	08/11/1916	09/11/1916
War Diary	Martinsart Wood	11/11/1916	12/11/1916
War Diary	Paisley Avenue	14/11/1916	14/11/1916
War Diary	Warloy	15/11/1916	15/11/1916
War Diary	Cezaincourt	17/11/1916	17/11/1916
War Diary	Volkerinckhove.	18/11/1916	29/11/1916
Miscellaneous			
Heading	117th Brigade. 39th Division. 1/16th Battalion Notts & Derby Regiment December 1916		
War Diary	Volkerinckhove	01/12/1916	11/12/1916
War Diary	Poperinghe	12/12/1916	12/12/1916
War Diary	Ypres	13/12/1916	13/01/1917
War Diary	Brandhoek.	14/01/1917	23/01/1917
War Diary	Ypres.	25/01/1917	30/01/1917
War Diary	Haslar House	01/02/1917	04/02/1917
War Diary	Ypres.	04/02/1917	04/02/1917
War Diary	Railway Wood	05/02/1917	05/02/1917
War Diary	Ypres.	07/02/1917	07/02/1917
War Diary	Railway Wood	09/02/1917	12/02/1917
War Diary	Ypres.	13/02/1917	13/02/1917
War Diary	E Camp.	15/02/1917	26/02/1917
War Diary	Zillebeke.	27/02/1917	03/03/1917
War Diary	Barracks Ypres	04/03/1917	10/03/1917
War Diary	Toronto Camp.	11/03/1917	14/03/1917
War Diary	Zillebeke.	15/03/1917	19/03/1917
War Diary	Barracks Ypres.	21/03/1917	26/03/1917
War Diary	Winnipeg Camp.	27/03/1917	02/04/1917
War Diary	Barracks Ypres.	03/04/1917	04/04/1917
War Diary	Sanctuary Wood.	06/04/1917	11/04/1917
War Diary	Brandhoek.	14/04/1917	14/04/1917
War Diary	Merckeghem	14/04/1917	26/04/1917

Type	Location	From	To
War Diary	L Camp.	27/04/1917	27/04/1917
War Diary	Brandhoek.	28/04/1917	30/04/1917
War Diary	Brandhoek. "O" Camp.	01/05/1917	14/05/1917
War Diary	Hill Top Sector.	15/05/1917	15/05/1917
War Diary	Canal Bank.	16/05/1917	22/05/1917
War Diary	Hill Top Sector.	23/05/1917	31/05/1917
War Diary	Brandhoek. "O" Camp.	31/05/1917	31/05/1917
Miscellaneous	Headquarters, 117th Infantry Brigade.	28/05/1917	28/05/1917
War Diary	O Camp Near Brandhoek.	01/06/1917	07/06/1917
War Diary	Wieltje. St. Jean.	08/06/1917	08/06/1917
War Diary	Wieltje	09/06/1917	15/06/1917
War Diary	Yser Canal Bank	16/06/1917	21/06/1917
War Diary	Hill Top	24/06/1917	30/06/1917
War Diary	Serques.	01/07/1917	22/07/1917
War Diary	Near Brandhoek Hill. Top Sector	28/07/1917	31/07/1917
War Diary	Hill Top	31/07/1917	31/07/1917
Operation(al) Order(s)	16th Battalion Sherwood Foresters. Operation Order No. 36	24/07/1917	24/07/1917
Miscellaneous	Time Table Barrage		
War Diary	St Julien	01/08/1917	07/08/1917
War Diary	Lacoqde Paille	07/08/1917	18/08/1917
War Diary	Ridge Wood	20/08/1917	22/08/1917
War Diary	Hollebeke	23/08/1917	25/08/1917
War Diary	Bois Confluent	27/08/1917	27/08/1917
War Diary	Ontario Camp	29/08/1917	30/08/1917
War Diary	Ontario Camp Near Reminghelst	02/09/1917	21/09/1917
War Diary	Curragh Camp	23/09/1917	25/09/1917
War Diary	Ridge Wood.	26/09/1917	26/09/1917
War Diary	Wakefield Huts Camp Near Locre	27/09/1917	31/10/1917
War Diary	Godazonne Farm.	01/11/1917	30/11/1917
War Diary	St Jean	01/12/1917	07/12/1917
War Diary	Abeele	08/12/1917	09/12/1917
War Diary	Quesques & Verval	10/12/1917	28/12/1917
War Diary	Seninghem	29/12/1917	29/12/1917
War Diary	Alberta	30/12/1917	31/12/1917
War Diary	Steenbeek	01/01/1918	06/01/1918
War Diary	Dambre Camp	07/01/1918	14/01/1918
War Diary	Canal Bank	15/01/1918	21/01/1918
War Diary	Road Camp.	21/01/1918	23/01/1918
War Diary	Suzanne	24/01/1918	30/01/1918
War Diary	Railway Camp Heudecourt	30/01/1918	31/01/1918
War Diary	Heudecourt	03/02/1918	28/02/1918
Heading	117th Inf. Bde. 39th Div. War Diary 16th Battn. The Sherwood Foresters (Nottinghamshire And Derbyshire Regiment.) March 1916		
War Diary	Dessart Wood Camp	01/03/1918	20/03/1918
War Diary	Sorel Le Grand.	21/03/1918	21/03/1918
War Diary	Longueval.	22/03/1918	22/03/1918
War Diary	Mont. St. Quentin.	23/03/1918	23/03/1918
War Diary	Clery.	24/03/1918	24/03/1918
War Diary	Herbecourt.	25/03/1918	26/03/1918
War Diary	Progart.	26/03/1918	26/03/1918
War Diary	Morcourt.	27/03/1918	27/03/1918
War Diary	Cayeux.	28/03/1918	28/03/1918
War Diary	Aubercourt.	29/03/1918	29/03/1918
War Diary	Hangard	30/03/1918	30/03/1918

War Diary	Longnej.	31/03/1918	31/03/1918
War Diary	Recques.	01/05/1918	23/05/1918
War Diary	Mentque.	24/05/1918	25/07/1918
War Diary	Nordausques	26/07/1918	29/07/1918
Heading	66th Division Training Cadres 39 Div 16th Bn Sherwood Foresters 1918 Aug 1919 June 39 Div 117 Bde. served Will 197 Bde L Of C From Sept 1918		
Heading	War Diary Of 16th Bn. Sherwood Foresters. From August 1st. 1918 To August 31st 1918 (Volume 3)		
War Diary	Nordausques.	01/08/1918	15/08/1918
War Diary	Abancourt	16/08/1918	21/08/1918
War Diary	Quesnes.	23/08/1918	31/08/1918
Heading	War Diary Of 16th. Sherwood Foresters. From 1st September 1918 To 30th. September 1918		
War Diary	Quesnes	01/09/1918	29/09/1918
Heading	War Diary Of 16th. Bn. Sherwood Foresters. From 1st October, 1918 To 31st. October, 1918		
War Diary	Quesnes.	02/10/1918	29/10/1918
Heading	War Diary Of 16th. Battalion Sherwood Foresters. From:- 1st. Novr. 1918 To:- 30th. Novr. 1918		
War Diary	Quesnes	02/11/1918	30/11/1918
War Diary	Haudricourt Reinforcement Camp.	01/12/1918	29/12/1918
War Diary	Aumale.	01/01/1919	09/01/1919
War Diary	Le Havre	15/01/1919	02/05/1919
War Diary	Sanvic	02/05/1919	02/05/1919
War Diary	Le Havre	04/05/1919	22/05/1919

Woods 2/5/11
Last 5/7/11

117th Brigade.
39th Division.

(CHATSWORTH RIFLES)

Battalion disembarked HAVRE 7.3.16.

1/16th BATTALION

NOTTS & DERBY REGIMENT

MARCH 1916

Army Form C. 2118

WAR DIARY
or
INTELLIGENCE SUMMARY

117/30.

10th Batt. Sherwood Foresters
(Chatsworth Rifles)

(Erase heading not required.)

Instructions regarding War Diaries and Intelligence Summaries are contained in F.S. Regs., Part II. and the Staff Manual respectively. Title Pages will be prepared in manuscript.

Place	Date	Hour	Summary of Events and Information	Remarks and references to Appendices
WITLEY CAMP	6/3/16	7.am	Left WITLEY CAMP for HAVRE via SOUTHAMPTON	
HAVRE	7/3/16	8.am	Landed at HAVRE (snowing hard) passed the night REST CAMP.	
HAVRE	8/3/16	8.25.am	Left HAVRE (GARE DES)	
STEENBECQUE	9/3/16	4.am	Arrived STEENBECQUE STATION, 39th DIVISION forms part of 1st Army, commanded by GEN. SIR. C. MONRO. G.C.B.	
"	10/3/16			
"	11/3/16			
"	12/3/16			
"	13/3/16	9.am	March from STEENBECQUE to ESTAIRES, inspected en route by LIEUT. GEN. SIR W.P. PULTENEY K.C.B. D.S.O. Commanding III CORPS 1st ARMY.	
DUMP HOUSE SAILLY	14/3/16	10.am	March from ESTAIRES to DUMP HOUSE near SAILLY, accomodated in BILLETS	
"	15/3/16			
"	16/3/16	3.pm.	Inspected by GEN SIR. C. MONRO. G.C.B. Commanding 1st ARMY	
"	17/3/16			
"	18/3/16			
ESTAIRES	19/3/16	10.am	March from SAILLY to ESTAIRES attached to 23rd BRIGADE, 6th DIVISION.	

WAR DIARY or INTELLIGENCE SUMMARY

Army Form C. 2118

16th Batty Sherwood Foresters (Chatsworth Rifles)

Place	Date	Hour	Summary of Events and Information	Remarks and references to Appendices
ESTAIRES	19/3/16		"A" & "B" Coys move into trenches near LAVENTIE, for instruction with 2nd Bn WEST YORKSHIRE REGT.	Working parties were finished on these days
"	20/3/16		35 men transferred to 181st TUNNELLING COY RE	
"	20/3/16		1 man "B" Coy wounded in the trenches	
"	21/3/16		1 man "A" Coy wounded in the trenches	
"	22/3/16		"A" & "B" Coys relieved in trenches near LAVENTIE by "C" & "D" Coys who were attached for instruction with the 2nd SCOTTISH RIFLES.	
"	23/3/16			
"	24/3/16		"C" & "D" Coys relieved (no casualties during tour in trenches)	
"	25/3/16			
"	26/3/16			
"	27/3/16	12. Noon.	COMMANDING OFFICER, ADJUTANT proceed BETHUNE to visit 20th Bn ROYAL FUSILIERS ANNEQUIN SOUTH.	
"	28/3/16	3.pm	Battalion arrives at BETHUNE and comes under orders of G.O.C. 33rd DIVISION billeted in BETHUNE.	

Army Form C. 2118

WAR DIARY
or
INTELLIGENCE SUMMARY

16th Bn. Sherwood Foresters
(Chatsworth Rifles)

(Erase heading not required.)

Place	Date	Hour	Summary of Events and Information	Remarks and references to Appendices
BETHUNE	29/3/16	11 a.m.	BATTALION march to ANNEQUIN SOUTH and comes under orders of G.O.C. 19th BRIGADE for training by companies in the AUCHY SECTION.	
ANNEQUIN SOUTH	29/3/16	5.30 a.m	"A & B" Companies move into trenches in AUCHY SECTION for instructions with 20th BN. ROYAL FUSILIERS	
"	30/3/16	6 p.m.	"C & D" Companies relieve "A & B" Companies in trenches AUCHY SECTION.	

Wilson Alpey Lieut Colonel
Comdg 16th Bn. Sherwood Foresters
(Chatsworth Rifles)

117th Brigade.
39th Division

1/16th BATTALION

NOTTS & DERBY REGIMENT

APRIL :1 9 1 6

Vol 2
xxxix
2.A.
M.M.

Army Form C. 2118

WAR DIARY
or
INTELLIGENCE SUMMARY

16TH (SER) BATTN. SHERWOOD FORESTERS.
(CHATSWORTH RIFLES).

(Erase heading not required.)

Instructions regarding War Diaries and Intelligence Summaries are contained in F. S. Regs., Part II. and the Staff Manual respectively. Title Pages will be prepared in manuscript.

Place	Date	Hour	Summary of Events and Information	Remarks and references to Appendices
AUCHY	1-4-16	7. P.M.	Battalion takes over the AUCHY RIGHT subsection from 20TH BN. ROYAL FUSILIERS	
"	2-4-16		2nd Lieut. H.L. MORELL wounded by rifle grenade, 1 man killed, 4 men wounded (rifle grenades)	
"	3-4-16		6 men wounded (1 shrapnel, 5 rifle grenades)	
"	4-4-16		1 Sergeant "A" Coy wounded by rifle grenade. Battalion relieved in the AUCHY RIGHT subsection by the 1/5TH SCOTTISH RIFLES	
	5-4-16		REST at BETHUNE	
	6-4-16		Battalion marches from BETHUNE to BUSNETTES near GONNEHEM	
BUSNETTES	7-4-16		In rest billets	
	8-4-16		do	
	9-4-16		do	
	10-4-16	10 a.m.	Inspection by Lt. GEN. SIR. R.C. HAKING, K.C.B. at GONNEHEM. REPORT RECEIVED from H.Q. 33RD DIVISION, from BRIG.-GENERAL P.W. ROBERTSON commanding 19TH INFANTRY BRIGADE	
			REPORT ON 16TH NOTTS & DERBYS attached to 19TH INFANTRY BRIGADE	
			OFFICERS. "A good keen lot, they are fortunate in having such a good Commanding Officer and Second in Command	
			N.C.Os. A far better stamp than in most of the New Army battalions	
			MEN. A very tough lot. Good physique generally."	

Army Form C. 2118

WAR DIARY
or
INTELLIGENCE SUMMARY

16TH (SER) BATTN. SHERWOOD FORESTERS
(CHATSWORTH RIFLES).

(Erase heading not required.)

Instructions regarding War Diaries and Intelligence Summaries are contained in F. S. Regs., Part II. and the Staff Manual respectively. Title Pages will be prepared in manuscript.

Place	Date	Hour	Summary of Events and Information	Remarks and references to Appendices
BUSNETTES	6.4.16		DISCIPLINE } GOOD. The Officers seem to have their men well in hand. MORALE } SANITATION } Satisfactory ORGANISATION } "I consider from what I have seen that this is a good battalion and well commanded. They seem to have a good system of work and organisation, and only require further experience." SD. F.W. ROBERTSON, Brig. General. Comdg. 19TH INFANTRY BRIGADE.	
	10.4.16		Remarks by Lt. Gen SIR R.C. HAKING. K.C.B. on foregoing report. "These reports are satisfactory. The 16th Notts and Derby Regt. seem to be a particularly good Battalion" 2nd Lt N.C. DAWSON transferred to command Light Trench Mortar Battery. 117th.	
BUSNETTES.	12.4.16			
	13.4.16			
	14.4.16			
	15.4.16		BRIG. GENERAL R.D.F. OLDMAN D.S.O. succeeds BRIG GENERAL P. HOLLAND. C.B. in Command of 117th INFANTRY BRIGADE	
	16.4.16. 9.45am		Battalion proceeds from BUSNETTES to RIEZ DU VINAGE	
RIEZ DU VINAGE	17.4.16. 6.pm.		Draft of 45 men from 19th RESERVE BATTALION arrive from ETAPLES	
"	18.4.16. 10.am.		BRIG. GENERAL R.D.F. OLDMAN D.S.O. inspects BATTALION in billets	
"	20.4.16. 10.am.		C.O. visits C2 subsection FESTUBERT line.	

WAR DIARY or INTELLIGENCE SUMMARY

Army Form C. 2118

16TH (SER) BATTN. SHERWOOD FORESTERS (CHATSWORTH RIFLES).

Place	Date	Hour	Summary of Events and Information	Remarks and references to Appendices
RIEZ DU VINAGE	21.4.16	1.30 p.m.	35 NCOs & men sent on permanent mining fatigue to FERME DU ROI near BETHUNE	
			LIEUT. R.F. DUNN and 35 oR attached to Machine Gun Corps	
	22.4.16		1 man wounded whilst attached to 13th GLOSTERS working party	
			14 men attached to O.C. FOREST CONTROL at LA MOTTE AU BOIS	
FESTUBERT	23.4.16	9.30 a.m.	Battalion proceeds from RIEZ DU VINAGE to the trenches, C2 subsection FESTUBERT LINE which comprises the ISLAND LINE. Battalion reds en route in 17th K.R.R.	
"			Billets in LES CHOUQUAX	
"	24.4.16		Enemy guns, our sniper gets a victim	
"	25.4.16	6 am	One man accidentally wounded in Island 14.	
"		9 p.m.	"Z" Company join up Islands 22 & 21, Sergeant W.A. EDWARDS killed.	
"			2nd Lt E.E. EDWARDES joins, posted to "A" Company.	
"	26.4.16		Sergeant Major DRUMMOND wounded.	
"	27.4.16		Batts relieved by 17th KINGS ROYAL RIFLES & proceeds to FESTUBERT in support	
	28.4.16		350 men detailed as working party for R.E.	
Nr DE L'ÉPINETTE	29.4.16		2nd Lieut H. CHAPPELL joins, posted to "D" Coy, 2nd Lieut E.A. LIFETREE joins posted to "B" Coy. Enemy shell & MG fire to one of "Z" Coys hills, one man wounded, one man slightly hurt.	
	30.4.16			

LIEUT. COLONEL,
COMMANDING 16th SERVICE Bn. SHERWOOD FORE TERS,
(CHATSWORTH RIFLES).

117th Brigade.
39th Division.

1/16th BATTALION

NOTTS & DERBY REGIMENT

M A Y 1 9 1 6

Army Form C. 2118

XXXIX

WAR DIARY
or
INTELLIGENCE SUMMARY

16TH (SER) BATTN. SHERWOOD FORESTERS.
(CHATSWORTH RIFLES).

(Erase heading not required.)

Instructions regarding War Diaries and Intelligence Summaries are contained in F.S. Regs., Part II. and the Staff Manual respectively. Title Pages will be prepared in manuscript.

Vol 3

G.A.

Place	Date	Hour	Summary of Events and Information	Remarks and references to Appendices
RUE DE L'EPINETTE	1-5-16	10.43 p.m.	Battalion relieves 17th K.R.Rifles in C2. SUB SECTION FESTUBERT.	
FESTUBERT	2-5-16		One man slightly wounded (at duty)	
	3-5-16			
	4-5-16			
	6-5-16	10.55 P.M.	Battalion relieved by 17th K.R.Rifles in C2. SUB SECTION FESTUBERT and proceeded to LE TOURET in reserve.	
LE TOURET	6-5-16 *			*: 350 men detailed for working parties under R.E. each day.
	7-5-16 *			
	8-5-16 *		2nd Lieut B.E. GARLAND joins Battalion	
	9-5-16		Battalion proceeds to RIEZ DE VINAGE. 117th BRIGADE in reserve	
RIEZ DE VINAGE	10-5-16		REST.	
	11-5-16		"	
	12-5-16		"	
	13-5-16		"	
	14-5-16			

Army Form C. 2118

WAR DIARY
or
INTELLIGENCE SUMMARY
(Erase heading not required.)

16TH (SER) BATTN. SHERWOOD FORESTERS.
(CHATSWORTH RIFLES).

Instructions regarding War Diaries and Intelligence Summaries are contained in F.S. Regs., Part II. and the Staff Manual respectively. Title Pages will be prepared in manuscript.

Place	Date	Hour	Summary of Events and Information	Remarks and references to Appendices
RIEZ DU VINAGE	15-5-16		REST	
	16-5-16		"	
GIVENCHY	17-5-16		Battalion took over B2. sub section at GIVENCHY relieving 1st CAMBRIDGESHIRE REGT.	
	18-5-16			
	19-5-16		3 men Killed (shell fire), 1 man accidentally drowned attached to 15th GLOUCESTERS mining party. 6 men wounded (rifle grenades)	
	20-5-16		7 men wounded (rifle grenades)	
	21-5-16		2nd Lieut C.N. Lipton, Sergeant Belcher, Killed, (rifle grenades) 2 men wounded (rifle grenades)	
	22-5-16		Battalion relieved in B2. sub section by 17th K.R. Rifles. Battalion in support in VILLAGE LINE	
	23-5-16		3 men killed (2 T.M) (1. B.W) 3 men wounded, (1. B.W, 1 H.E Shell, 1 T.M.)	
	24-5-16		Three men wounded (1 returned to duty)	
	25-5-16		Battalion relieves 17th K.R Rifles in B2. sub section GIVENCHY	
	26-5-16		One man killed (rifle grenade) few men wounded, (rifle bullet, 9 rifle grenades) 4 at duty	

1875 Wt. W593/826 1,000,000 4/15 J.B.C. & A. A.D.S.S./Forms/C. 2118.

WAR DIARY
or
INTELLIGENCE SUMMARY
(Erase heading not required.)

Army Form C. 2118

16TH (SER) BATTN. SHERWOOD FORESTERS
(CHATSWORTH RIFLES).

Place	Date	Hour	Summary of Events and Information	Remarks and references to Appendices
GIVENCHY	26.5.16		Captain W.G. CONSTABLE proceeds to ENGLAND on leave	
	27.5.16		One man killed, two wounded. (rifle grenades)	
	28.5.16		2nd Lieut A.D. PERKIN and seventy men wounded (rifle grenade) 3 at duty.	
	29.5.16		2 men killed. Whizz bangs, 5 men wounded (2 whizz bangs) (2 rifle grenades) (1 accidentally) Battalion relieved in B2 SUB SECTION by 17th K.R.R. and proceed in reserve to GORRE.	
GORRE	30.5.16			
	31.5.16		One man wounded (at duty)	

[signature]
LIEUT. COLONEL

[stamp: COMMANDING 16th (SERVICE) BATTN. SHERWOOD FORESTERS (CHATSWORTH RIFLES)]

117th Brigade.
39th Division.

1/16th BATTALION

NOTTS & DERBY REGIMENT

JUNE 1916

WAR DIARY or INTELLIGENCE SUMMARY

Army Form C. 2118 — Vol 4 — June

16TH (SER) BATTN. SHERWOOD FORESTERS (CHATSWORTH RIFLES).

XXIX

Place	Date 1916	Hour	Summary of Events and Information	Remarks and references to Appendices
GORRE	June 3rd		Battalion relieves 17th Bn. K.R.R. in B2 SUB SECTION GIVENCHY. New Battalion Headquarters at SOUTH MOOR VILLA occupied.	4.A
GIVENCHY	" 4th		OPERATIONS. Relief carried out satisfactorily under cover of Patrol. Artillery quiet on both sides. Intermittent rifle grenade activity during the night and at "STAND TO" this morning to which we replied with vigour. Enemy machine guns – indirect fire – played at intervals during the night on buildings at and across WINDY CORNER – GIVENCHY ROAD.	
"	"		CASUALTIES. 2 men killed, (one R.G) one R.B.), 5 men wounded (two N.F, three R.G.)	
"	" 4th	10 P.M.	The Battalion carried out a successful Bombing Raid on the German trenches SOUTH of DUCKS BILL on the night of JUNE 4th. The Bombing Party consisting of 4 Officers and 70 other ranks left our trenches in accordance with predrawn up plans. The first party under 2nd Lieut R.C. DAVIES was held up and German wounded, bombed before reaching the German wire causing a number of casualties. They succeeded however and entered the German trench through the gap cut in the wire at the spot indicated slowly followed by the second party under Lieut. A. HARDY. The first party pushed about 60 yards to the right, the second party about 60 yards to the left and Lewis the communication trenches. One third party under the second party followed aid	

2nd Lieut. J.R. CHOLERTON acting as a Bomb Party followed

Army Form C. 2118

WAR DIARY or INTELLIGENCE SUMMARY

16TH (SER) BATTN. SHERWOOD FORESTERS
(CHATSWORTH RIFLES)

(Erase heading not required.)

Place	Date 1916	Hour	Summary of Events and Information	Remarks and references to Appendices
GIVENCHY	June 4th		established themselves in the German trench. On the first party being checked outside the enemy wire a message was sent back for the fourth or Reserve party under Lieut BRADWELL located in our front line trench to reinforce and support the left company. This was successfully done. The Germans that mostly taken to ground and were in their dug-outs. Two or seven dug-outs full of Germans were bombed. After occupying the German trenches for about half an hour the order was given to withdraw. The withdrawal was well carried out in an orderly manner, strong pegs being left on each flank. Three Germans were bayonetted and about 20 killed or drowned in dug-outs. A grenade rifle stand was demolished and some equipment taken. CASUALTIES Our casualties were :- One Officer wounded (2nd LIEUT R.C DAVIES) Other Ranks, 2 killed, 5 missing, and 18 wounded. These except for 2nd LIEUT R.C DAVIES all occurred before entering the German trench. The whole party showed an admirable spirit, worked well and kept their heads. I wish however specially to notice the services of the following Officers and Other Ranks:- 2nd LIEUT R.C DAVIES. This Officer had previously reconnoitred the line of advance. He led the first party with great skill and dash, he was just in the enemy's trench, entered a dug-out and pulled out a German prisoner. He was one of the last to leave the enemy trench, and was unfortunately severely	

Army Form C. 2118

WAR DIARY or INTELLIGENCE SUMMARY

16TH (SER) BATTN. SHERWOOD FORESTERS (CHATSWORTH RIFLES)

(Erase heading not required.)

Instructions regarding War Diaries and Intelligence Summaries are contained in F.S. Regs., Part II. and the Staff Manual respectively. Title Pages will be prepared in manuscript.

Place	Date 1916	Hour	Summary of Events and Information	Remarks and references to Appendices
GIVENCHY	June 4"		wounded during the retirement when removing the German wires. I would recommend his services be recognised by immediate award.	
"	"		LIEUT. A. HARDY handled his party extremely well and showed dash and enterprise.	
"	"		2nd LIEUT. J.R. CHOLERTON who was in command of the forward liason party, worked with coolness and courage. He maintained communication between the night and left parties and with the party in our front two trench. He was responsible for the removal of the wounded and replenishment of bombs and generally for the withdrawal.	
"	"		No. 26665. SERG. BRADNELL. S. showed great coolness and bravery. Particularly in repulsing a hostile bombing party of 3 men and one left whom he forced to take cover in a dugout, he followed them up and bombed them into silence in the dugout. He subsequently assisted to carry 2nd LIEUT. R.C. DAVIES during the withdrawal.	
"	"		No. 26276. SERG. WYATT. A. This N.C.O. handled his men with skill and courage until he was severely wounded. He has on several occasions previously rendered good service when in charge of patrols and wiring parties.	
"	"		No. 26719. PTE. BOWLER. L. was leading bayonet man of No.1 party and throughout	

Army Form C. 2118

WAR DIARY
or
INTELLIGENCE SUMMARY
(Erase heading not required.)

16TH (SER) BATTN. SHERWOOD FORESTERS (CHATSWORTH RIFLES).

Place	Date 1916	Hour	Summary of Events and Information	Remarks and references to Appendices
GIVENCHY	JUNE 4th		The operation was constantly getting to grips with the enemy. We entered two dug-outs and bayonetted 3 Germans and displayed great bravery. No.26652. Pte CHILVERS H.H. This man's services were specially brought to my notice by 2nd Lieut R.C. DAVIES, before his removal to hospital. His coolness and courage were conspicuous throughout the operation.	
	JUNE 5th		DIVISIONAL THANKS. GEN. SIR. C. MONRO COMDG. 1st ARMY, SIR R.C. HAKING, COMDG. XI CORPS, sent to the COMMANDING OFFICER and OFFICERS comments and congratulated them on the success of the operation. EXTRACT from D.R.O. dated JUNE 6th 1916.— The MAJOR GENERAL Comdg. congratulates the 117th INFANTRY BRIGADE on the successful raid on the night of 4/5th JUNE. He also congratulates the 16th BATTALION SHERWOOD FORESTERS on being the first unit in the Division to enter the enemy trenches.	
	JUNE 5th		OPERATIONS. Enemy artillery between 7.45.a.m and 8.45.a.m today. Not heavy. T.M. shells fell in the neighbourhood of PICCADILLY. Enemy rifle grenade activity commenced 1.30 pm. until 2.15 pm. At 5.30 pm. in answer to rifle grenades fired by us, enemy sent over a considerable number, we retaliated and silenced him. Rifle grenade activity continued during the night, and our Officers	

WAR DIARY or INTELLIGENCE SUMMARY

Army Form C. 2118

16TH (SER) BATTN. SHERWOOD FORESTERS
(CHATSWORTH RIFLES)

Place	Date	Hour	Summary of Events and Information	Remarks and references to Appendices
GIVENCHY	JUNE 5th		OPERATIONS CONTD. Patrol went out at dusk from SAP. K to examine the N end of the NORTH CRATER. Patrol was unable to proceed very far owing to the water which is pumped from the mines. The ground in front of SCOTTISH TRENCH is very marshy. CASUALTIES. One man killed (B.W.) six men wounded. (one B.W. 5 rifle grenades) 2nd LIEUTS. STEVENSON A, SEABROOK N.S, WILLIAMS T.C.O, HILL S.N, SIMPSON O.M, BENNER W, GODWIN L.W. joined the Battalion	
	JUNE 6th		OPERATIONS. Desultory rifle grenade activity throughout the day, we replied at intervals with good effect. Battalion relieved by the 1st CAMBRIDGESHIRE REGT in B2 SUB SECTION and proceeded	
ESSARS	JUNE 7th		to ESSARS in Divisional Reserve where two companies bivouaced for the night. Battalion marched to VILLES in LES CHOCQUAUX.	
LES CHOCQUAUX	" 8th		LIEUT. COLONEL C. HERBERT SIBBNEY proceeds to ENGLAND on leave.	
"	" 10th		Draft of 22 N.C.Os and men arrived from 19th (Res) Battalion.	
"	"		MAJOR GENL. R. DAWSON. C.B. assumes command of the 39th DIVISION vice MAJOR GENL. N.W. BARNARDISTON M.V.O. to ENGLAND.	
LE TOURET	" 11th		Battalion proceeded in Reserve at LE TOURET.	
"	" 13th		LIEUT. G.N.E. STRONG proceeded to ENGLAND. One man wounded on working party.	
"	" 14th		MAJOR H.M. MILWARD appointed to command 17th BATTN SHERWOOD FORESTERS.	

Army Form C. 2118

WAR DIARY
or
INTELLIGENCE SUMMARY

(Erase heading not required.)

16TH (SER) BATTN. SHERWOOD FORESTERS
(CHATSWORTH RIFLES)

Place	Date 1916	Hour	Summary of Events and Information	Remarks and references to Appendices
LE TOURET	JUNE 14		MAJOR N. HOUGHTON appointed Second in Command of the Battn. Vice MAJOR. H.M. MILWARD. CAPTAIN. N.G. CONSTABLE assumed Command of "D" COMPANY. " J.G. COOKE " " " "B" "	
	JUNE 15th		LIEUT COLONEL C. HERBERT STEPNEY returned from Leave LIEUT. A.D. PAPKIN rejoined Battalion after being wounded 2nd LIEUT. A.L. HOLLAND wounded on working party our PERTUBERT ISLANDS LIEUT D.W. STEVENS proceeded to ENGLAND on leave	
	JUNE 16th		Draft of 18 N.C.Os and men arrived from 19th (Res) Battalion Draft of 25 N.C.Os and men arrived from 11th Battn SHERWOOD FORESTERS Battalion relieves 20th BATTN LANCASHIRE FUSILIERS in the FERME DU BOIS RIGHT SUB SECTION.	
FERME DU BOIS	" 17th		OPERATIONS. At 17.30 am fire was directed on a working party heard N. of FERME DU BOIS.	
	" 16th		OPERATIONS. Our snipers have been active throughout the day. They claim 2 periscopes and 3 Germans, one of the latter was hit at dawn working at FERME COUR D'AVOUE, his body could be seen for some time. The enemy later pushed red sandbags in front of it. Another was shot in a communication trench while carrying sand and was carried away by the remainder of the party. The others were fired at as the front line trench, three appeared to be hit. At about 9 pm our artillery trenches the enemy parapet at S22.C.H.6, This fire was kept under fire by our Lewis Guns during the night.	

Army Form C. 2118

WAR DIARY
or
INTELLIGENCE SUMMARY
(Erase heading not required.)

16TH (SER) BATTN. SHERWOOD FORESTERS
(CHATSWORTH RIFLES).

Place	Date 1916	Hour	Summary of Events and Information	Remarks and references to Appendices
FERM. DU BOIS	JUNE 18		OPERATIONS. CONT? The Lewis Guns also fired in the direction of S.22.c.5.9. where a patrol had reported a working party. An Officers patrol went out from the post S.21.b.9.5. at 10.30 pm returning at 11.50 pm. CASUALTIES. Two men wounded (Rifle bullet).	
	" 19TH		OPERATIONS. Only sniping activity during the day. Four periscopes were hit. Our Lewis Guns were active during the night and claim to have dispersed a working party at S.22.a.4.8. A fixed rifle firing on N. corner of FERME COUR D'AVOUE was fired at intervals, this drew considerable Machine Gun fire from the enemy from 11.30 pm until daybreak. An Officers patrol went out at 10.30 pm. MAJOR N. HOUGHTON proceeded to AMIENS on leave. 2nd LIEUT. A. SCRAGG joined the Battalion. CASUALTIES. 4 men wounded (Rifle bullet)	
	" 20TH		OPERATIONS. The enemy showed very much less activity during the day, on the other hand at night there was a marked increase of machine gun and rifle fire. They were especially active after midnight, we replied with Lewis Guns. Our snipers claim 5 victims and in 3 cases the evidence is good. Periscopes were fired at, but as they are put very low it is difficult to see whether they are broken, in two instances they were taken down after a shot was fired.	

Army Form C. 2118

WAR DIARY or INTELLIGENCE SUMMARY

16TH (SER) BATTN. SHERWOOD FORESTERS (CHATSWORTH RIFLES)

Place	Date 1916	Hour	Summary of Events and Information	Remarks and references to Appendices
FERME. DU BOIS.	JUNE 20.		CASUALTIES. 3 other ranks wounded. (Rifle Bullets) DIVISIONAL GENERAL'S THANKS. The following letter signed by MAJOR GENERAL R. DAWSON. C.B. Comdg 39th DIVISION dated June 20th/16 was received today. "The General Officer Commanding the 39th Division has read with much interest the report of the reconnaissance made by LIEUT P.U.KAYS, 2nd LIEUT CHAPPELL F.H. L/C. NEEDHAM & PTE MARRIOTT, 16TH BN SHERWOOD FORESTERS on the night of 16/19th JUNE, and wishes to let them know that he thinks it was a very good bit of work and tidily executed." "A" & "B" Coys relieved "C" & "D" Coys respectively in FERME DU BOIS SUB SECTION.	
	JUNE 21.		OPERATIONS. Between 9 and 10am the enemy fired H."77 Shells near CADBURY, BOURNVILLE & NEW BREASTWORK, it is possible that he saw our working party. At 8 to 10.p.m the fired 8 shells on to the front line near bays 68 to 74, no damage. Our snipers shot two men, their bodies were seen before they were carried away, two others are believed to have been hit. New work seen at S22, a.8.8. was kept under fire from our Lewis guns during the night.	
	"23".		CASUALTIES. 2 other ranks wounded. (Rifle Bullets). OPERATIONS. Enemy have been very quiet, less machine fire activity than on the previous night.	

WAR DIARY
or
INTELLIGENCE SUMMARY

Army Form C. 2118

16TH (SER) BATTN. SHERWOOD FORESTERS
(CHATSWORTH RIFLES)

Place	Date 1916	Hour	Summary of Events and Information	Remarks and references to Appendices
FERME DU BOIS	June 22.		OPERATIONS	

Our Lewis Guns have been active in firing on suspected machine guns. Snipers claim one victim and one periscope, but the enemy have been forced to take down periscopes on four occasions and to close his loopholes whenever they were found to be open. Three practice patrols went out.

Our snipers continued active.

In answer to a notice which was put up near the FERME COUR D'AVOUE "WHY FIRE WHEN PEACE IS SO NEAR". They shot three of the enemy.

DECORATIONS.

The Commanding Officer has much pleasure in notifying that HIS MAJESTY the KING, has been pleased to award the following decorations.

2nd LIEUT R.C. DAVIES. MILITARY CROSS

No 26665. Sergt. S. BRADWELL. DISTINGUISHED CONDUCT MEDAL

" 26719. Pte. L. BORLER. MILITARY MEDAL.

These are the first Honours won by any N.C.Os and men who came out with the 39th DIVISION. The Commanding Officer feels sure that all ranks will join with him in congratulating most heartily the recipients. He hopes that these Honours will be the forerunner of many others gained by the CHATSWORTH RIFLES

WAR DIARY or INTELLIGENCE SUMMARY

Army Form C. 2118

16TH (SER) BATTN. SHERWOOD FORESTERS (CHATSWORTH RIFLES)

Place	Date 1916	Hour	Summary of Events and Information	Remarks and references to Appendices
FERME DU BOIS	June 23		**OPERATIONS.** Enemy shelled our front line with .77 shells at 11.30 a.m., noon, 1 p.m. and between 4 & 5 p.m. Two shells also fell behind the front line at 12.15 circa. On the first occasion he obtained three direct hits on our front line parapet but otherwise no damage was done. Our shelling on the salient at S.22.C. had excellent effect, several hits on the support trenches where the enemy had been recently working were obtained. Owing to the large amount of work done by the enemy on the night of the 21st & 22nd no practice patrols were sent out, but our Lewis guns showed great activity. Snipers claim 3 victims, and with continuous evidence, and two periscopes. **CASUALTIES** One man killed, one man wounded. (Rifle bullet).	
	"24th		**OPERATIONS.** Very little hostile artillery or rifle fire by day or night. Enemy put over right of QUINQUE RUE what appeared to be a Trench Mortar about 2 p.m. yesterday. Three of the enemy exposed themselves on our left front, one of whom was hit by our snipers, his body was carried away. An Officers patrol, LIEUT. P.V. LAWS. went out from RIGHT Coy at 11-15 p.m. LIEUT. P.V. LAWS. returned slightly wounded in forehead. **CASUALTIES.** One officer wounded (LIEUT. P.V. LAWS) two other ranks wounded.	
	"25th		**OPERATIONS.** The day was marked by considerable artillery activity over our right coy front and also on batt flanks. In the morning from 9 a.m. to	

WAR DIARY
or
INTELLIGENCE SUMMARY
(Erase heading not required.)

Army Form C. 2118

16TH (SER) BATTN. SHERWOOD FORESTERS. (CHATSWORTH RIFLES).

Place	Date 1916	Hour	Summary of Events and Information	Remarks and references to Appendices
FERME DU BOIS	JUNE 25th		OPERATIONS. 12 noon the right company sector was lightly shelled with 77 shells, none however fell nearer than 40x behind the front line. The enemy snipers were very inactive during the day and there was little movement in their trenches. They are undoubtedly keeping their heads down. An Inter-company relief was carried out last night between the front and support lines. A German who showed himself above the parapet for a few moments was shot by our snipers and fell back into the trench. He was wearing a dark blue tunic and cap, the latter with a red band round it and a small peak. Two periscopes were also destroyed. At about 2 a.m. an enemy working party near the FERME COUR D'AVOUÉ was seen, fired upon and dispersed. CASUALTIES. NIL. 2nd LIEUT. F.H. GOSLING joins the Battalion.	
	26th		OPERATIONS. There was considerable artillery activity during the day, mostly on our part. Between 1pm & 1.15 pm the enemy put about 20 shells on PRINCES ROAD, several of which failed to explode. There was slightly more rifle and machine gun fire than the night before, especially at stand to this morning. Our Officers Patrol (2nd LIEUT F.H. CHAPPELL)	

WAR DIARY
INTELLIGENCE SUMMARY

Army Form C. 2118

16TH (SER) BATTN. SHERWOOD FORESTERS. (CHATSWORTH RIFLES).

Place	Date 1916	Hour	Summary of Events and Information	Remarks and references to Appendices
FERME DU BOIS	JUNE 26th		**OPERATIONS.** Went out from the left Company to examine the ditches between our front line and the FERME COUR D'AVOUE. At 7.10.pm a man's head was seen above the parapet at S.22.a.6.3. and was shot by our snipers. He was wearing a forage cap. LIEUT. D.W. STEVENS returned from leave. **CASUALTIES.** One man wounded (Rifle bullet). 2ND LIEUT. A. SCRAGG accidentally wounded.	
	27th		**OPERATIONS.** The enemy were exceedingly quiet throughout the day. Between 9.45.a.m. and 10.15.a.m. 13 "77" shells fell just behind the front line on the extreme left of our sector, but no damage was done. Our Artillery retaliated on the enemy parapet. The victim is claimed by our sniper. **CASUALTIES.** One man killed (Rifle bullet).	
	28th		**OPERATIONS.** Between 8 and 10 am the enemy shelled new BREASTWORK, putting over about 20. "77" shells, no damage was done. In the afternoon it.pm. + 5.pm the four lines of RIGHT Coy was systematically traversed from QUINQUE CROSSING to RUE de CAILLOUX with light shells, doing a little damage in one or two places. At about 8 pm the enemy was observed to be mending two parapets at S.22.a.8.6. where it had been damaged by our Artillery fire was also opened and work ceased. Sniper claim one German. Enemy snipers were exceedingly quiet, only	

WAR DIARY or INTELLIGENCE SUMMARY

Army Form C. 2118

16TH (SER) BATTN. SHERWOOD FORESTERS. (CHATSWORTH RIFLES)

Place	Date 1916	Hour	Summary of Events and Information	Remarks and references to Appendices
FERME DU BOIS	JUNE 28th		OPERATIONS. An occasional shot being fired. The night was very quiet.	
			CASUALTIES. One man wounded (Rifle bullet).	
	29th		OPERATIONS. Our guns continued their activity during yesterday with but little response from the enemy. About 6. a.m. 4. "7 shells fell near BOURNVILLE STATION, and in the afternoon from 4 to 5. pm there was shelling in the neighbourhood of the RUE DU BOIS just to the left of CADBURY TRENCH. Gas was discharged by R.E's from QUINQUE CROSSING at 12 midnight and at 12.30 a.m. all clear was given. No retaliation. The night was quiet with little machine gun fire. An Inter-Company relief was carried out & completed by 11.25. pm. Two germans were seen walking just behind their front line near the FERME COUR D' AVOUE, our snipers shot once and the first German was seen to fall. His friend quickly jumped into the trench and disappeared from view. Both men were wearing long tan greatcoats with round blue caps. During the afternoon our artillery shelled NORBERT ALLEY, and one shell was seen to burst on the SALLY PORT at this point. We also shot down a periscope. The enemy snipers were again active excepting at dusk when a number of shots were fired, we thereupon fired at several of	

Army Form C. 2118

WAR DIARY or INTELLIGENCE SUMMARY
(Erase heading not required.)

16TH (SER) BATTN. SHERWOOD FORESTERS.
(CHATSWORTH RIFLES).

Instructions regarding War Diaries and Intelligence Summaries are contained in F.S. Regs., Part II. and the Staff Manual respectively. Title Pages will be prepared in manuscript.

Place	Date 1916	Hour	Summary of Events and Information	Remarks and references to Appendices
FERME DU BOIS	JUNE 29th		OPERATIONS. Their loophole which seemed to give them. CASUALTIES. 2 men wounded (rifle bullet)	
	30th		OPERATIONS. On the attack by the BOAR'S HEAD by the 116th INFANTRY BRIGADE in conjunction with the operations we created a smoke barrage from our front line by means of P. Bombs and smoke candles, commencing at 2.50 am and ceasing about 3-25 am. Five minutes after the commencement of our bombardment, the enemy started shelling our front line, reaching the parapet at many points (on the LEFT Coy front 10 Coys). He also opened fire with machine guns. A number of heavy R.E. Shells dropped between the front line and BOURNVILLE, so far only 4 or 5 casualties have been reported. At 3-5am we opened fire with Vickers Lewis guns and continued at intervals. As soon as our guns opened fire on the left the enemy sent up a number of red rockets and later on green rockets were sent up. About 5 am 28/29th June three or four Germans were seen working behind their front line close to MULBERRY ALLEY. our snipers dispersed them with rifle fire. At 1.15m. a German sniper was observed firing through a loophole, we fired several steel piercing bullets, penetrating the loophole and knocking down two sandbags overhead. During the day several 77 shells struck the front making gaps in the parapet in six places. Our casualties were 1 man killed & 5 men wounded. Over stretch Ranks trough in wounded four NO MANS LAND	

1875 Wt. W503/826 1,000,000 4/15 J.B.C. & A. A.D.S.S./Forms/C. 2118.

WAR DIARY
or
INTELLIGENCE SUMMARY

Army Form C. 2118

Place	Date	Hour	Summary of Events and Information	Remarks and references to Appendices
FERME DU BOIS	JUNE 30. 1916		His Grace the DUKE of DEVONSHIRE has written congratulating the Battalion on the honours gained in the recent raid. His Grace hopes to visit the Battalion in France before his departure from ENGLAND to take up his post as GOVERNOR GENERAL of CANADA.	

Charles Hope Lt Col
16th Sherwood Foresters.

117th Brigade.
39th Division.

1/16th BATTALION

NOTTS & DERBY REGIMENT

JULY 1916

WAR DIARY or INTELLIGENCE SUMMARY.

Army Form C. 2118.

16TH (SER.) BATTN. SHERWOOD FORESTERS.
(CHATSWORTH RIFLES).

Place	Date	Hour	Summary of Events and Information	Remarks and references to Appendices
FERME DU BOIS	1916 JULY 1ST		**OPERATIONS.** Between 8am and 8·30am about 20 "77" shells fell in the vicinity of our Battalion Headquarters. No damage was done. About 9.30am 6 shells fell right of CADBURY TRENCH near RUE DE BOIS otherwise there has been no artillery activity since the previous night operation and remarkably little machine gun & rifle fire. At 12.30am last night one of our listening patrols on the right Coys front came back and reported that a party of the enemy variously estimated between 10 & 15 men were approaching our wire. They were then about 50x out or 10x from the listening post. A Lewis Gun was quickly fetched and in conjunction with rifle fire the enemy was dispersed. Several of them were seen to get up and run towards their own lines. Two Officer patrols under CAPTAIN P.H. COLERIDGE and 2/LIEUT BOVER went out. **CASUALTIES.** One man suffering from shell shock. LIEUT MAXMILAN JACKSON joins the Battalion.	

Army Form C. 2118.

WAR DIARY
or
INTELLIGENCE SUMMARY.

No 2.

16TH (SER) BATTN. SHERWOOD FORESTERS
(CHATSWORTH RIFLES).

(Erase heading not required.)

Place	Date	Hour	Summary of Events and Information	Remarks and references to Appendices
FERME DU BOIS.	1916 JULY 2nd		**OPERATIONS.** With the exception of the following slight hostile shelling the day was quiet. 6 am to gain occasional rounds of shrapnel over our supports and RUE DE BOIS. Noon to 12.30. Woolley Bears near junction of CADBURY & FRONT LINE. 4 pm to 4.30 several "77 shells on Right Coy near QUINQUE CROSSING. The last named made three small gaps in our parapet otherwise no damage was done. At dusk we sent out a fighting patrol from our Right Coy to engage if possible any enemy patrol which might be out. An enemy sniper was shot by our snipers. The German method of work was to wear a black mask over his head and fire over the top of black sandbags on the parapet so that at the range at this point (400 yards) it was exceedingly difficult to spot him. One of our snipers laid in wait all morning until his position was given away by the flash of his rifle. Our man is convinced that he obtained a clean hit through the head, as the German was seen to fall forward his rifle canting upwards. **CASUALTIES.** One man killed, one man wounded (Rifle bullets).	

WAR DIARY
or
INTELLIGENCE SUMMARY.

Army Form C. 2118.

16TH (SER) BATTN. SHERWOOD FORESTERS.
(CHATSWORTH RIFLES).

Place	Date	Hour	Summary of Events and Information	Remarks and references to Appendices
FERME DU BOIS.	1916 JULY 3rd		**OPERATIONS.** The last 24 hours have been very quiet. In the afternoon between 3 & 3.40 pm a few shells fell in rear of the right Coy, and about 11 pm ROPE ST and TUBE STATION were lightly shelled for a few minutes. No damage. A fighting patrol under 2/LIEUT BOWER was sent out by the left Coy but no enemy patrols were encountered. An inter-company relief was carried out and completed by 11-45. pm. Snipers claim to have hit a German. This man was wearing a khaki coloured cap with a yellow metal badge in the form of a grenade. **CASUALTIES** one man wounded (Rifle bullet).	
	JULY 4TH		**OPERATIONS.** Between 6 & 6.15 pm about 100 "77" shells fell just to the left of CADBURY, otherwise there was little hostile shelling during the day. A fighting patrol under 2/LIEUT BENNER went out from the right Coy, but was unable to engage the enemy. Our snipers have been worrying the enemy. Two attempts made by German snipers to fire over the parapet were stopped. In another case a fixed rifle was spotted and fired at. At "Cloud Do" this morning a German was seen walking along the parapet	

Army Form C. 2118.

WAR DIARY
or
INTELLIGENCE SUMMARY.
(Erase heading not required.)

No. 7.   16TH (SER) BATTN. SHERWOOD FORESTERS.
(CHATSWORTH RIFLES)

Instructions regarding War Diaries and Intelligence Summaries are contained in F.S. Regs., Part II. and the Staff Manual respectively. Title pages will be prepared in manuscript.

Place	Date	Hour	Summary of Events and Information	Remarks and references to Appendices
FERME DU BOIS	JULY 4TH		**OPERATIONS, Contd.** Three shots were fired but the light was bad and the result doubtful. Our guns shelled the enemy front line just S. of QUINQUE CROSSING and made a gap in the parapet at S.22.c.6.6. We left this under heavy gun fire during the night. **CASUALTIES.** 5 other ranks accidently wounded including one at duty.	
	JULY 5TH		**OPERATIONS** There was slight artillery activity in the morning when some .77 shells fell behind the left Coy. front line and a few on the right. The latter made two gaps in the parapet of Bays 3 & 4. Between 3 & 3.30 pm CADBURY TRENCH and TUBE STATION each received a few shells, doing no damage. During the night there was rather more machine gun activity than usual and the QUINQUE RUE was repeatedly searched. A fighting patrol which was out from 10.15 pm to 2.30 am, succeeded in locating a hostile listening post. At 6.30 pm our snipers observed water being baled out of the enemy trench by means of buckets. A man was seen to show his head and shoulders during this work and was finally brought down by our man. We also broke one periscope and fired successfully at a loophole just	

Army Form C. 2118.

WAR DIARY
or
INTELLIGENCE SUMMARY.

No. 5. 16TH (SER) BATTN. SHERWOOD FORESTERS
(CHATSWORTH RIFLES).

(Erase heading not required.)

Place	Date	Hour	Summary of Events and Information	Remarks and references to Appendices
FERME DU BOIS	1916 JULY 5th		OPERATIONS. Cont. to the left of SALLY PORT causing it to be closed up.	
			CASUALTIES. 3 men wounded (Rifle bullets).	
	JULY 6TH		OPERATIONS. Except for a few stray '77 shells the day was very quiet. During the operations at GIVENCHY last night the enemy shelled LEGRETT the right of our front line, two gaps were made in our parados and one casualty occurred. At 1035 STATION a dugout was knocked in. A fighting patrol under 2/LIEUT HART was out from 10.45pm until 2.30.a.m but no enemy patrols or working parties encountered. At 1.15a.m the enemy bombed the hedge N.W. of the FERME COUR D'AVOUE where our the previous night our patrol had halted and discovered an enemy listening post. Enemy snipers have been considerably more active the last two days. They have been firing from several loopholes previously unused, and have also fired over the parapet. Our snipers have shot into several loopholes and it is thought that good execution has been done. It is possible that a local relief has taken place. A man who showed his head and shoulders over the parapet at stand to this morning was shot by us.	

Army Form C. 2118.

WAR DIARY
or
INTELLIGENCE SUMMARY.

No. 6.

16TH (SER) BATTN, SHERWOOD FORESTERS.
(CHATSWORTH RIFLES).

(Erase heading not required.)

Place	Date	Hour	Summary of Events and Information	Remarks and references to Appendices
FERME DU BOIS	1916 JULY 6th		CASUALTIES. Two other ranks wounded. (one at duty) CAPTAIN W.G. CONSTABLE promoted MAJOR LIEUT A. HARDY " CAPTAIN 2/LIEUT C.G. LORD " LIEUTENANT 2/LIEUT J.R. CHOLERTON " LIEUTENANT	
	JULY 7th		OPERATIONS At 10.45 a.m. about 20 whizz bangs fell near Battalion Heargrs and down the RUE DU BOIS. Our snipers were very busy yesterday, two Germans were definitely hit, the evidence in each case being reliable and 3 or 4 other doubtful hits are recorded. Six Snipers were accounted for. In view of the increased hostile sniping activity of the last two days we have been right down the line and put two or three steel piercing bullets into every loophole that could be spotted. A fighting patrol under LIEUT BOWER was sent out from 10.30pm to 2.30am. No hostile patrols encountered. Our men succeeded in getting close up to the German wire and threw some bombs into their trenches, groans were heard immediately afterwards. The front line received a few 77 shells	

WAR DIARY
or
INTELLIGENCE SUMMARY.

Army Form C. 2118.

16TH (SER) BATTN. SHERWOOD FORESTERS (CHATSWORTH RIFLES).

No. 7.

Place	Date	Hour	Summary of Events and Information	Remarks and references to Appendices
FERME DU BOIS	1916 JULY 7th		OPERATIONS Cont. during the day and about 7p.m. one fell on the SALLY PORT nr. the Left Coy frontage doing a little damage. An inter-company relief was carried out and completed by 11.35 p.m. MAJOR N. HOUGHTON returns from leave. CASUALTIES. Two men wounded (rifle bullets).	
	JULY 8th		OPERATIONS. The last 24 hours have been very quiet excepting for the enemy machine guns which were active during the night. A German who showed his head and shoulders close to QUINQUE CROSSING was shot through the body by our snipers and was seen to tumble backwards into the trench. He was wearing the ordinary field grey uniform. Two binoculars were broken. A reconnoitring patrol under 2nd LIEUT SEABROOM examined NO MANS LAND and the enemy wire opposite S.W.O.1. A second patrol was sent out to protect the reconnoitring patrol and engage any enemy patrols encountered. CASUALTIES. One man killed. (rifle bullet)	
	JULY 9th		OPERATIONS. Between 1.30 and 2.30 p.m. the enemy shelled CADBURY TRENCH, NEW BREASTWORK, COW KEEP and the TROCODERA O.P. (RUE DU BOIS).	

Army Form C. 2118.

WAR DIARY
or
INTELLIGENCE SUMMARY.
(Erase heading not required.)

No 8. 16TH (SER) BATTN. SHERWOOD FORESTERS.
(CHATSWORTH RIFLES).

Place	Date	Hour	Summary of Events and Information	Remarks and references to Appendices
	1916.			
FERME DU BOIS	JULY.9th		OPERATIONS, cont'd.	
			We eventually retaliated, but at about 3.15 the enemy started again on our front line left Coy. putting 25 whizz bangs over but no damage was done. At 10pm we sent out a fighting patrol under 2nd LIEUT STEVENSON. No enemy patrols were encountered and men therefore went up to the German wire and threw bombs into their front line. Our air patrol was returning the enemy opened heavy machine gun and rifle fire causing us two casualties, otherwise the night was quiet. At about 8.30 a.m. a man was observed behind the German lines at S.22.B.o.3. Our snipers fired at him & he was seen to fall.	
			CASUALTIES. 3 men wounded. (1 Shrapnel, 2 Rifle bullets.)	
	JULY.10th		OPERATIONS Between 9.30 & 10 a.m. the enemy shelled with H.E the NEW BREASTWORK RUE DU BOIS and DEAD COW. At 4.45 p.m. about 25 whizz bangs fell on the right Coy front trenching the parapet in 3 places and in the neighbourhood of ROPE KEEP, otherwise the day was quiet. There was little machine gun or rifle fire during the night. About 11.p.m the RUE DU BOIS was again shelled lightly. Our snipers shewn two returns the evidence co...	

WAR DIARY
or
INTELLIGENCE SUMMARY.
(Erase heading not required.)

Army Form C. 2118.

16TH (SER) BATTN. SHERWOOD FORESTERS.
(CHATSWORTH RIFLES).

No. 9.

Place	Date	Hour	Summary of Events and Information	Remarks and references to Appendices
FERME DU BOIS	1916 JULY 10TH		OPERATIONS. Cont'd in each case being conclusive. One periscope broken. A fighting patrol under LIEUT J. BROWN was out from 10.30pm to 1.30am. A working party was heard just N. of FERME COUR D'AVOUE and a number of bombs were thrown into their midst. CASUALTIES. NIL.	
	JULY 11TH		OPERATIONS. The enemy shelled the front line of left Coy between 6 and 9am, & again about 9.30am. Gas whizz bangs fell on front line causing slight damage to one of our bays. Between 3 and 6pm the enemy shelled junction of NEW BREASTWORK & CADBURY. Our Artillery and trench mortars were registering between 3 & 4pm. This drew retaliation on front line of right Coy. No damage was done. There was little machine gun or rifle fire during the night. Our snipers claim to have broken two periscopes. A fighting patrol under 2nd LIEUT SIMPSON was out from 11.30pm to 2.30am. No enemy patrols were encountered. CASUALTIES. Two men killed, (1 shell & 1 Rifle bullet,) one man wounded (T.M).	

Army Form C. 2118.

WAR DIARY or INTELLIGENCE SUMMARY.

(Erase heading not required.)

16TH (SER) BATTN. SHERWOOD FORESTERS.
(CHATSWORTH RIFLES).

No. 10.

Place	Date	Hour	Summary of Events and Information	Remarks and references to Appendices

FERME DU BOIS	1916 JULY 12th		**OPERATIONS.** A very quiet day except between 1-30 and 2.30 a.m. Between 8 and 12 noon a few whizz bangs fell near NEW BREASTWORK and CADBURY. Between 1.30 and 2.30 a.m. enemy retaliates on left Coy front for bombardment by us on the night with whizz bangs causing slight damage to parapets. At 1-20 a.m. our Artillery and Trench Mortars opened fire on enemy lines round S.22.c.45.55. Enemy retaliated immediately with artillery and Trench Mortars on our front line & Communication trenches, parapet breached in several places on RIGHT Coy frontage. About 1 a.m. about 200 4.2 shells fell near TUBE STATION. Our snipers claim to have hit 3 periscopes. The following is a report on the raid carried out on the German trenches at S.22.C.45.65. morning of July 12th/16.
			
			 (1) OBJECTIVE. To touch enemy trenches at S.22.C.45.65. on a front of 160 yds.
			 (2) COMPOSITION. 1 Officer 17 Other Ranks
			                      1st Party 1 " 17 "
			                      2" " 1 " 17 "
			                      3rd " 1 " 17 "
			                      Reserve 1 " 10 "
			
			 continued	

Army Form C. 2118.

WAR DIARY
or
INTELLIGENCE SUMMARY.
(Erase heading not required.)

16TH (SER) BATTN. SHERWOOD FORESTERS.
(CHATSWORTH RIFLES)

No 11.

Place	Date	Hour	Summary of Events and Information	Remarks and references to Appendices
FERME DU BOIS	1916. JULY 12TH		RAID. Continued.	

(3) The parties had orders to cross our parapet and lie down in NO MAN'S LAND ready to advance at the prearranged time on completion of our bombardment.

No1 party advanced and entered the enemy trenches through the gap cut in the wire by our French Mortars. They turned to the left for about 50 yards. Six Germans were bayonetted and four dugouts full of Germans were bombed successfully, one dugout being set on fire. Two German Officers were seen to take cover in one of the above dugouts. The party then set out in search for more bombs, but found they were unsupported, neither of the other parties having entered the trenches. They therefore withdrew, taking the wounded with them. The Officer in charge of the second party unfortunately lost connection with the first party early in the operation and appears to have completely lost his bearings. This regrettable occurrence prevented what otherwise might have proved a successful operation. As it was the first party claim to have accounted for about 40 of the enemy including two Officers. In addition many dead Germans were seen in the trenches who had been killed by our bombardment. The cutting of the German wire by our two new French Mortars was very

Continued

Army Form C. 2118.

WAR DIARY
or
INTELLIGENCE SUMMARY.
(Erase heading not required.)

16TH (SER) BATTN. SHERWOOD FORESTERS
(CHATSWORTH RIFLES)

Place	Date	Hour	Summary of Events and Information	Remarks and references to Appendices
FERME DU BOIS	1916 July 12th		RAID Continues was very well carried out. Our casualties were not unduly heavy considering the severity of the enemy barrage, and as far as can be at present ascertained are:— 2nd Lieut SEABROOK wounded & missing. Lieut CHOLERTON wounded, two Other ranks killed & 18 other ranks wounded. I much regret that 2nd Lieut SEABROOK who led the first party with great gallantry and still is wounded and is missing. CASUALTIES in RAID. Lieut J.R. CHOLERTON. Wounded. 2nd " H.S. SEABROOK Missing & believed killed 2nd " N.C. DAWSON Died of wounds Other ranks one killed, two missing believed killed, and 21 wounded including 5 at duty. CASUALTIES Since RAID:— 2nd Lieut C.J. HART wounded. Other Ranks 2 killed, + 13 wounded, including 2 at duty. 2nd LIEUT N.C. DAWSON attached to 117th Trench Mortar Battery died of wounds received whilst serving two gun under heavy bombardment.	

Army Form C. 2118.

WAR DIARY
or
INTELLIGENCE SUMMARY.
(Erase heading not required.)

**16TH (SER) BATTN. SHERWOOD FORESTERS.
(CHATSWORTH RIFLES).**

No. 13.

Place	Date	Hour	Summary of Events and Information	Remarks and references to Appendices
FERME DU BOIS	1916 JULY 12th		FURTHER REPORT ON RAID of JULY 12th.	
			With further reference to my report of this date on the raid carried out by my Battalion on July 12th, it has since been ascertained that the Germans were impressed. I beg to bring to your notice for favourable consideration the following names:- 2nd LIEUT. HARRY SPENCER SEABROOK. This Officer had previously reconnoitred the ground. He led his party with great skill and displayed conspicuous gallantry. He was first man in the trenches, bayonetted two Germans and continued to lead his men until he fell. No. 25699 Sergt. HILDRETH A.G. took charge of the party when 2nd LIEUT SEABROOK became a casualty. He displayed coolness and courage, organizing attacks on enemy dug-outs and continued the Officer's work. The supply of bombs ran out. Only when it was definitely established that the party was unsupported and lacked further supplies of bombs did he order the withdrawal, which he conducted with resource and ability taking the wounded with him. No. 25812 Pte HUTCHINSON. J. and 25863 Pte PEGG T.E. displayed conspicuous gallantry. They were among the first to enter the German trench. When the supply of bombs ran out they returned to the dump of bombs at the German wire	continue

Army Form C. 2118.

WAR DIARY
or
INTELLIGENCE SUMMARY.
(Erase heading not required.)

**16TH (SER) BATTN. SHERWOOD FORESTERS.
(CHATSWORTH RIFLES).**

No. 14.

Instructions regarding War Diaries and Intelligence Summaries are contained in F.S. Regs., Part II. and the Staff Manual respectively. Title pages will be prepared in manuscript.

Place	Date	Hour	Summary of Events and Information	Remarks and references to Appendices
FERME DU BOIS	1916 July 12th		under heavy fire & brought back a supply of bombs which they took from our casualties. On their return they followed up a party of six or seven Germans and bombed them in their dugouts getting it or five. No.25737 Pte. A.B. CLEMENTS was with 2nd LIEUT SEABROOK on entering the German trench. He displayed conspicuous gallantry & devotion to duty. He acted as bayonet man and accounted for two Germans, and continued to fight as leading bayonet man after 2nd LIEUT SEABROOK became a casualty, until killed himself. 2nd LIEUT A. SCRAGG rejoined after being wounded.	
	July 13th		OPERATIONS. A very quiet day. Between 6.45 & 7.15. pm enemy shelled junction of CADBURY TRENCH and RUE DU BOIS. At 12.30 pm a few whizz bangs fell to the left of CADBURY TRENCH. Enemy shelled our RIGHT COY with whizz bangs intermittently during the day. They are apparently fired from an enfilade battery on our right. The night was remarkably quiet with machine gun & rifle fire. At 10-15 am about 150 yds to the left of FERME COUR D'AVOUE a German was seen in a shell hole in enemy's front line parapet. He was	

Army Form C. 2118.

WAR DIARY
or
INTELLIGENCE SUMMARY.
(Erase heading not required.)

16TH (SER) BATTN. SHERWOOD FORESTERS.
(CHATSWORTH RIFLES).

Place	Date	Hour	Summary of Events and Information	Remarks and references to Appendices
FERME DU BOIS	JULY 13th 1916		OPERATIONS Cont: Wearing a flack mask. Three shots were fired at him by our sniper, he was noticed to fall forward & was carried away. A fighting patrol under LIEUT. R.L. ILLINGWORTH was out from 11.pm to 3.a.m. No hostile patrols were encountered & no movements were heard in enemies line. CONGRATULATIONS. One Officer and 18 other ranks of the raiding party were inspected at LOISNE by GEN. SIR. C. MONRO. G.C.B on July 13th and congratulated by him on their success. CASUALTIES. 5 men wounded including 2 at duty.	
	JULY 14		OPERATIONS. Exceptionally quiet day, except between 11 & 12 pm. At 11.pm in reply to our Artillery's shots the enemy retaliate on our left company with whizz bangs and Trench Mortars. Fire ceased at 11.40.pm, no damage caused. Enemy also shelled our night company heavily between 11 & 11.30 pm chiefly with whizz bangs. Parapet hit in several places. Enemy fired on our retaliation. Our Artillery apparently registering in enemy front line trenches near BOARS HEAD. At 6.20 pm about 20 whizz bangs fell in and near TUST STATION, little damage was done. Again at 10.25 pm a few whizz bangs fell near Coy Headquarters.	

Army Form C. 2118.

WAR DIARY
or
INTELLIGENCE SUMMARY.
(Erase heading not required.)

16TH (SER) BATTN. SHERWOOD FORESTERS.
(CHATSWORTH RIFLES).

N° 16.

Instructions regarding War Diaries and Intelligence Summaries are contained in F.S. Regs., Part II. and the Staff Manual respectively. Title pages will be prepared in manuscript.

Place	Date	Hour	Summary of Events and Information	Remarks and references to Appendices
FERMÉ DU BOIS	1916 July. 14th		OPERATIONS. Cont. Considerable machine gun and rifle fire commenced on our bombardment on the left and lasted for about 1½ hours. At about 6 p.m. two Germans were seen to look over trench at S.22.a.8.4. One probably an Officer wearing soft brown collar & tie & peaked cap with soft grey top and broad white band, the other wore a cap with grey top & broad white band. At 7 p.m. a man appeared at same position, he was fired at by our snipers and disappeared quickly, apparently shot. Enemy snipers very quiet all day until 6.p.m. when their loopholes were open. Our snipers fired several rounds of steel piercing ammunition into them & loopholes were closed. An Officers patrol under 2nd LIEUT D.W. STEVENS was out from 10.50 pm to 2.a.m. CASUALTIES. Two men wounded.	
	July. 15th		OPERATIONS. The day passed quietly. Between 4 & 4.35 pm 22 whizz bangs fell about 100 yards in rear of NEW BREASTWORK. At 5.p.m. 25. 5.9 shells fell near NEW BREASTWORM & CADBURY TRENCH, the latter was slightly damaged. During the night considerable enemy machine gun fire on our parapet near FERME DU BOIS. Our Lewis guns & machine guns fired on Gap A3 in enemy wire.	

Army Form C. 2118.

WAR DIARY
or
INTELLIGENCE SUMMARY.
(Erase heading not required.)

**16TH (SER) BATTN. SHERWOOD FORESTERS.
(CHATSWORTH RIFLES).**

No. 17.

Instructions regarding War Diaries and Intelligence Summaries are contained in F.S. Regs., Part II. and the Staff Manual respectively. Title pages will be prepared in manuscript.

Places	Date	Hour	Summary of Events and Information	Remarks and references to Appendices
FERME DU BOIS.	1916. JULY. 15th		OPERATIONS. Contd. Enemy snipers very quiet during the day. Our sniper claim to have hit 5 periscopes. An Officer patrol was out from 11 p.m. to 2 w.t a.m. no enemy parties or enemy patrols encountered. CASUALTIES. NIL.	
	JULY. 16TH		OPERATIONS. A very quiet day. About 4.15 p.m. about 5 whizz bangs fell behind parapet at S.6.2. Very little machine gun or rifle fire during the night and exceptionally quiet. Enemy snipers again inactive. Our snipers claim one victim and to have smashed 4 periscopes. All enemy loopholes were fired at and hit with steel piercing ammunition. An Officer patrol under 2nd LIEUT C.E. GARLAND was out from 11.30 p.m. to 1.45 a.m. CASUALTIES. One man wounded. (Rifle bullet).	
	JULY. 17th		OPERATIONS. The day passed very quietly. Our artillery were very active on our right front. Very little machine gun or rifle fire during the night, slight artillery activity on our part. Enemy snipers considerably more active. Our snipers claim to have smashed 4 periscopes. Enemy loopholes fired at during the day along the whole of our front.	

Army Form C. 2118.

WAR DIARY
or
INTELLIGENCE SUMMARY.

(Erase heading not required.)

No. 18.

16TH (SER) BATTN. SHERWOOD FORESTERS
(CHATSWORTH RIFLES)

Place	Date	Hour	Summary of Events and Information	Remarks and references to Appendices
FERME DU BOIS.	JULY 17th 1916.		OPERATIONS Contd. An Officers patrol under 2nd LIEUT. C.F. BOWER was out from 11.30.pm until 2.30.a.m. CASUALTIES. NIL. CAPTAIN W.P.H. MUNDEN. R.A.M.C. appointed to the STAFF for duty with D.D.M.S. 39TH DIVISION. LIEUT. S.I. LINDEMAN R.A.M.C. assumes medical charge of the Battalion vice CAPT. W.P.H. MUNDEN. The Commanding Officer wishes to express to CAPTAIN MUNDEN his appreciation of the constant care and devotion to duty he has always displayed during the past 8 months with the Battalion. He is sure all ranks will join in wishing him the best of good luck and congratulate him on his appointment.	
	JULY 18TH		OPERATIONS. Intermittent artillery activity throughout the day. Very little machine gun and rifle fire during the night. Good results were obtained by our snipers yesterday and four of the enemy accounted for and two periscopes smacked. Enemy snipers showed considerable activity throughout the day. An Officers patrol under 2nd O.E. GARLAND was out from 1.15.a.m to 2.15.a.m. CASUALTIES. NIL.	

Army Form C. 2118.

WAR DIARY
or
INTELLIGENCE SUMMARY.

No. 19.

16TH (SER) BATTN. SHERWOOD FORESTERS.
(CHATSWORTH RIFLES).

(Erase heading not required.)

Place	Date	Hour	Summary of Events and Information	Remarks and references to Appendices
FERME DU BOIS	JULY 19TH		**OPERATIONS.** A very quiet day passed. At 8 pm a few whizz bangs fell at head of CADBURY TRENCH. Enemy machine gun and rifle fire more active throughout the night. Our snipers were again successful, three of the enemy being accounted for, and three periscopes smashed. Enemy snipers were active during the afternoon. A patrol under 2ND LIEUT V.G.W.HILL was out from 11 pm to 1.45 am. **CASUALTIES.** NIL.	
	JULY 20TH		**OPERATIONS.** A very quiet day. At 10.40 pm in reply to our artillery on the right, several whizz bangs fell on our right company front. At 12.35 am the enemy retarded right of our front line with whizz bangs for about 10 minutes. The enemy ceased fire on our retaliation. At 12.45 am a few whizz bangs fell on FOSSE du BOIS. A good deal of enemy machine gun & rifle fire during the night. Our Artillery very active on right and left flanks during day and night. Enemy snipers very quiet. Our snipers claim to have hit three of the enemy and smashed 5 periscopes. A body under 2ND LIEUT F.H. CHAPPELL left our trenches at 9 x c.35.4.3 to attempt to capture a prisoner. CASUALTIES. One man killed (Rifle bullet).	

Army Form C. 2118.

WAR DIARY
or
INTELLIGENCE SUMMARY.
(Erase heading not required.)

No. 20.

16TH (SER) BATTN. SHERWOOD FORESTERS.
(CHATSWORTH RIFLES).

Place	Date	Hour	Summary of Events and Information	Remarks and references to Appendices
FERME DU BOIS	July 20/9/16		Battalion relieved in FERME DU BOIS Section by 12th & 13th Bn. ROYAL SUSSEX REGIMENT & became Battalion in reserve for the 118th Brigade with Headquarters at CANAL HOUSE near GORRE. Battalion billeted at TUNING FORM near GORRE.	
CANAL HOUSE GORRE	July 31st		The Commanding Officer wishes to place on record his appreciation of the soldierly spirit displayed by all ranks during their long tour of duty in the trenches in FERME DU BOIS section. The Battalion has been continuously in front line trenches for a period of 35 days. Although they have undertaken no offensive on a large scale the Battalion has been constantly engaged with the enemy. Patrols, listening posts & wiring parties have entered NO MANS LAND nightly. One successful raid has been carried out and much useful work has been done in strengthening and improving our defences. The cheerfulness with which all ranks have responded to the calls made on them and the excellent discipline maintained augurs well for the future of the Battalion. The Battalion incurred the following casualties during its tour. Killed 3 Officers & 17 Other Ranks. Wounded 4 Officers & 85 Other Ranks.	

Army Form C. 2118.

WAR DIARY
or
INTELLIGENCE SUMMARY.

16TH (SER) BATTN. SHERWOOD FORESTERS.
(CHATSWORTH RIFLES).

No 21.

(Erase heading not required.)

Place	Date	Hour	Summary of Events and Information	Remarks and references to Appendices
CANAL HOUSE. GORRE	JULY 23rd 1916		DECORATIONS. The Commanding Officer has much pleasure in notifying that His Majesty the King has been pleased to award the following decorations. No. 25812. Pte J. HUTCHINSON MILITARY MEDAL 25863 " T.E. PEGG - do - The Commanding Officer feels sure that all ranks will join with him in congratulating most heartily the recipients.	
BETHUNE	JULY 24th 1916		The Battalion proceeded to BETHUNE and took over billets at COLLEGE DES JEUNES FILLES as Battalion in reserve to 117th Brigade. 2ND LIEUT W.I. HASTINGS joins the Battalion.	
TUNING FORK.	JULY 26th		The Battalion proceeded to billets in TUNING FORK near GORRE and became Battalion in Brigade Reserve relieving 1/1 HERTS. Regt of the 118th Brigade.	
	JULY 27th		GEN. SIR. C. MONRO. G.C.B. presented MILITARY MEDAL RIBANDS to No 25812 Pte J. HUTCHINSON and No 25863 Pte T.E. PEGG. at MERVILLE.	
	JULY 29th		DECORATION. The Commanding Officer has much pleasure in notifying that HIS MAJESTY the KING has been pleased to award the following decoration. No 25699 Sergt HILDRETH. A.G. DISTINGUISHED CONDUCT MEDAL.	

Contd

Army Form C. 2118.

WAR DIARY
or
INTELLIGENCE SUMMARY.

No. 22.

16TH (SER) BATTN. SHERWOOD FORESTERS.
(CHATSWORTH RIFLES).

(Erase heading not required.)

Place	Date	Hour	Summary of Events and Information	Remarks and references to Appendices
TUNING FORK	JULY 29th 1916		The Commanding Officer feels sure that all ranks will join with him in congratulating most heartily the recipient.	
	JULY 31st		LIEUT P. V. LAWS rejoined the Battalion after being wounded.	
			Copy of letter received by No 25699 Sgt A. Hildick from BRIGADIER GENERAL R.D.F. OLDMAN. D.S.O. Commanding 117th Infantry Brigade.	
			"I am very pleased to be able to congratulate you on getting your D.C.M. Ever since the 16th Battalion Sherwood Foresters have first countenance with the enemy in his own trenches they have distinguished themselves. Your action was worthy of the highest praise and you very well deserved your decoration."	
			(Sd) R.D.F. OLDMAN. Comdg 117th Infantry Brigade.	

Lieut. Colonel,
Commanding 16th Service (R. Sherwood Foresters Regt)
(Chatsworth Rifles)

117th Brigade.
39th Division.

1/16th BATTALION

NOTTS & DERBY REGIMENT

AUGUST 1 9 1 6

Army Form C. 2118.

WAR DIARY
or
INTELLIGENCE SUMMARY.
(Erase heading not required.)

**16TH (SER) BATTN. SHERWOOD FORESTERS.
(CHATSWORTH RIFLES).**

No. 1.

Place	Date	Hour	Summary of Events and Information	Remarks and references to Appendices
GORRE.	AUG. 1st 1916.		Battalion relieved the 17th BN. KINGS ROYAL RIFLE CORPS in GIVENCHY left SUB SECTION with Battalion Headqrs at SOUTH MOOR VILLA.	
GIVENCHY.	" 2nd		OPERATIONS. The enemy fired three rounds from a Trench Mortar on to NORTHERN CRATERS FRONT at 3.a.m. Our retaliation was effective. A patrol under 2nd LIEUT. C.E. GARLAND went out from the left at 1.0 a.m. & returned at 3.45 a.m.	
			CASUALTIES. One man wounded. (Shrapnel)	
	" 3rd		OPERATIONS. Between 3 & 6 p.m., 70 to 80 5.9 Shells were fired on the right of the sector falling near "D" SAP, REGENT ST. & the houses at A.9.d.2.3. At 6 p.m 9 mm fano fell near FRENCH FARM and F. SAP. At 1.10 a.m. we exploded a small mine west of the craters already in existence S. of F. SAP. Craft party of 20 men went out, but it was found useless to consolidate. Enemy replied very promptly with rapid fire and a little rifle grenade and T.M. fire. Three salvoes of 77 were fired N. of KINGS ROAD.	
			CASUALTIES. 4 men wounded. (Rifle Grenade.)	

Army Form C. 2118.

WAR DIARY
or
INTELLIGENCE SUMMARY.

No. 2.   16TH (SER) BATTN. SHERWOOD FORESTERS
(CHATSWORTH RIFLES).

(Erase heading not required.)

Place	Date	Hour	Summary of Events and Information	Remarks and references to Appendices
GIVENCHY	Aug. 4th 1916.		OPERATIONS Enemy has been very quiet during last 24 hours only occasional rifle grenades were fired by him and one Trench Mortar. We fired about twice the number of rifle grenades and our T.M's fired behind the NORTHERN CRATERS & at A.10.C.1.7. At 4.p.m. our artillery made a short bombardment of the enemy trenches on the right of the sector and continued firing at intervals during the evening. They were made to provoke any retaliation. Two salvos of 7" H.E. shells which fell at 7.p.m. near GIVENCHY CHURCH appeared to be in reply to our T.M's which were registering at that time. The man was seen looking over their SPP opposite I.SAP. 4 was shot through the head by our snipers at a range of 40 yards.	
			CASUALTIES. One man wounded.	
	" 5th		OPERATIONS. Between 9.10.a.m. and T.M. bombs were fired on PICCADILLY between KINGS ROAD & REGENT ST & a few more were fired between 3 & 4 p.m.	
			CASUALTIES. One man killed and two wounded (Shrapnel)	

Army Form C. 2118.

WAR DIARY
or
INTELLIGENCE SUMMARY.
(Erase heading not required.)

16TH (SER) BATTN. SHERWOOD FORESTERS
(CHATSWORTH RIFLES).

No. 3.

Instructions regarding War Diaries and Intelligence Summaries are contained in F.S. Regs., Part II. and the Staff Manual respectively. Title pages will be prepared in manuscript.

Place	Date	Hour	Summary of Events and Information	Remarks and references to Appendices
GIVENCHY	Aug 6th 1916.		OPERATIONS. At 6:30 a.m. enemy shelled our lines behind PICCADILLY with 4.2 & 77 H.E. and shrapnel, about 10 rounds were fired. Our Artillery retaliated on CRATER TRENCH. A little damage was done by T.Ms to PICCADILLY. A trot T.M. duel occurred at 2:15 a.m., the enemy bombs falling near POPPY REDOUBT, and ours around SUNKEN ROAD TRENCH. CASUALTIES. 3 men wounded. RELIEF. The Battalion was relieved in the GIVENCHY left sub-section by the 1st Bn HANTS REGIMENT, & proceeded to billets in LE HAMEL & ESSARS.	
LE HAMEL	Aug 7th 1916.		CASUALTIES. One man killed (attached to 117th Light Trench Mortar Battery) and one man (shot in hospital) wounded during bombardment of BETHUNE	
	"6th"		Battalion tested in Gas Chamber at LE TOURET.	
	"9th"		Battalion marched to BETHUNE and were billeted at the ECOLE DES JEUNES FILLES	
BETHUNE	"10th"		Battalion marched from ECOLE DES JEUNES FILLES BETHUNE to AUCHEL.	

T2131. Wt. W708—776. 500000. 4/15. Sir J. C. & S.

Army Form C. 2118.

WAR DIARY
or
INTELLIGENCE SUMMARY.

No. 4.   16TH (SER) BATTN. SHERWOOD FORESTERS.
(CHATSWORTH RIFLES).

(Erase heading not required.)

Place	Date	Hour	Summary of Events and Information	Remarks and references to Appendices
AUCHEL	AUG. 11TH 1918.		The Battalion marched from AUCHEL to LA THIEULOYE and were inspected en route by MAJOR GEN. G.J. CUTHBERT. C.B.C.M.G. Commanding 39TH Division. The Battalion came under the orders of the 3RD Army, Commanded by Gen. Sir EDMUND ALLENBY, K.C.B. DECORATION. No. 26151. LANCE SERGEANT E. GILBERT. attached to the 117TH TRENCH MORTAR BATTERY awarded the "MILITARY MEDAL" for gallantry and devotion to duty.	
LA THIEULOYE	"14TH" "16TH"		Battalion commenced "BRIGADE TRAINING". LIEUT. R.L. WINGWORTH promoted CAPTAIN vice CAPTAIN F.A. BUTT transferred to 11TH BATTN. SHERWOOD FORESTERS with effect from JULY 25TH 1916. Under authority 39TH DIVISION pending publication of LONDON GAZETTE.	
	"22ND"		2ND LIEUT. W.R.A. LEHFELDT promoted LIEUTENANT with effect from JULY 25TH 1918. Under authority 39TH DIVISION pending publication of LONDON GAZETTE. LIEUT. R.H. ELLIS rejoined the Battalion from FOREST CONTROL 1ST ARMY. LIEUT. R.F. DUNN. proceeded to ENGLAND to report to G.O.C. Machine Gun Training Centre GRANTHAM.	

Army Form C. 2118.

WAR DIARY
or
INTELLIGENCE SUMMARY.
(Erase heading not required.)

No 5.   **16TH (SER) BATTN. SHERWOOD FORESTERS (CHATSWORTH RIFLES).**

Instructions regarding War Diaries and Intelligence Summaries are contained in F.S. Regs., Part II. and the Staff Manual respectively. Title pages will be prepared in manuscript.

Place	Date	Hour	Summary of Events and Information	Remarks and references to Appendices
LA THIEULOYE	Aug. 23rd 1916.		The Battalion continued march southwards from LA THIEULOYE and were billeted for the night at BUNEVILLE.	
BUNEVILLE	"24th"		Battalion marched from BUNEVILLE to NEUVILLETTE	
NEUVILLETTE	"25th"		Battalion marched to AUCHIE. The Battn. come under the orders of the Reserve Army (Commanded by Lieut Genl Sir H.de la P. GOUGH K.C.B.	
AUCHIE	"26th"		Draft of 50 men arrived from Base	
"	"28th"		Battalion marched from AUCHIE to BEAUSSART.	

Sept 1st 1916.

[signature]
LIEUT. COLONEL,
COMMANDING 16th SERVICE BN SHERWOOD FORESTERS,
(CHATSWORTH RIFLES).

117th Brigade.
39th Division.

1/16th BATTALION

NOTTS & DERBY REGIMENT

SEPTEMBER 1 9 1 6

Army Form C. 2118.

WAR DIARY
or
INTELLIGENCE SUMMARY.

16TH (SER) BATTN. SHERWOOD FORESTERS.
(CHATSWORTH RIFLES).

No. 1.

(Erase heading not required.)

Place	Date	Hour	Summary of Events and Information	Remarks and references to Appendices
BEAUSSART.	SEP. 1ST 1916.		Here it was learnt that the 39TH DIVISION would form part of the RESERVE ARMY Commanded by GEN. SIR. H. de la P. GOUGH. K.C.B. and came under the orders of LIEUT. GENERAL. A.E. FANSHAWE. C.B. (COMDG. V TH CORPS.	7.A.
	2ND		The 117TH BRIGADE moved from BEAUSSART and proceeded into the trenches in the BEAUCOURT- SECTOR with BRIGADE S BATTALION HEADQUARTERS at KNIGHTSBRIDGE, relieving the 118TH BRIGADE.	
BEAUMONT HAMEL.	3RD.		The 39TH DIVISION attacked the German trout line opposite BEAUMONT- HAMEL, NORTH of the RIVER ANCRE in conjunction with an attack by the 2ND ARMY DIVISIONS SOUTH of the RIVER ANCRE. The 39TH DIVISION order of battle was as follows:— 116TH BRIGADE on the RIGHT. 117TH " " " LEFT. 118TH " " " RESERVE. The 117TH BRIGADE attacked in the following order:— 16TH BN RIFLE BRIGADE RIGHT BATTN.	

Army Form C. 2118.

WAR DIARY
or
INTELLIGENCE SUMMARY.

No. 2

16TH (SER) BATTN. SHERWOOD FORESTERS
(CHATSWORTH RIFLES).

(Erase heading not required.)

Place	Date	Hour	Summary of Events and Information	Remarks and references to Appendices
BEAUMONT HAMEL	Sept 3rd 1916		OPERATIONS, Cont'd	
			LEFT BATTN 17TH BN SHERWOOD FORESTERS.	
			SUPPORT " 17TH " KINGS ROYAL RIFLES. CORPS	
			RESERVE " 16TH " SHERWOOD FORESTERS.	
			The attack started at 5.10 A.M. after a four minutes intense bombardment. The 17TH BN. SHERWOOD FORESTERS advanced successfully & gained the first and second German lines. The RIFLE BRIGADE initial attack was met by heavy fire and they failed to obtain their objective. Their Battalion was reformed and attacked again supported by the 17TH KINGS ROYAL RIFLES. They reached the German trenches but were unable to hold them. The 17TH SHERWOODS having their flanks exposed were also obliged to retire. The other units of the Division appear to have met with similar results. The 16TH BN SHERWOOD FORESTERS were employed chiefly as carrying parties for the two assaulting Battalions. Several of these carrying parties reached the German lines, in some instances making several journeys across NO MANS LAND. Others were engaged as trench	

Army Form C. 2118.

WAR DIARY
or
INTELLIGENCE SUMMARY.

(Erase heading not required.)

16TH (SER) BATTN. SHERWOOD FORESTERS (CHATSWORTH RIFLES).

No. 2. A.

Place	Date	Hour	Summary of Events and Information	Remarks and references to Appendices
BEAUMONT HAMEL	SEPT 3rd 1916		OPERATIONS Cont. Control Posts, and supplying forward dumps. This work was well carried out under a very heavy hostile artillery barrage. The casualties of the three Battalions of the 117th Brigade engaged in the assault were heavy, the losses in Officers being particularly severe. The casualties of the Battalion were as follows:— 2nd LIEUT. F.H. CHAPPELL — KILLED 2nd " J. BROWN — WOUNDED 2nd " W.J. HASTINGS — " 2nd " W. BENNER — " 2nd " O.M. SIMPSON — " OTHER RANKS 9 KILLED " 3 DIED OF WOUNDS " 8 MISSING " 78 WOUNDED. The attacks of the two Divisions South of the R. Ancre also failed.	

WAR DIARY or INTELLIGENCE SUMMARY.

Army Form C. 2118.

16TH (SER) BATTN. SHERWOOD FORESTERS (CHATSWORTH RIFLES).

No. 2. B.

Place	Date	Hour	Summary of Events and Information	Remarks and references to Appendices
BEAUMONT HAMEL	Sept 3rd/16.	10.30 pm	The Battalion was relieved by the 1/1 Cambridge Regt, 118th Brigade and were billeted for the night in MAILLY WOOD.	
	4th		The Battalion took over billets at BEAUCAMPS. Draft of 44 men joined the Battalion from 111th INFANTRY BASE DEPOT	

P.T.O.

Army Form C. 2118.

WAR DIARY
or
INTELLIGENCE SUMMARY.
(Erase heading not required.)

16TH (SER) BATTN. SHERWOOD FORESTERS
(CHATSW. RIFLES).

Place	Date	Hour	Summary of Events and Information	Remarks and references to Appendices
BEAUMONT HAMEL	Sept 8th 1916.		The N.C.O. became a casualty, made several journeys through the enemy keeping his party well together and keeping the forward dumps well supplied. He displayed gallantry and power of command & devotion to duty. No 7326 PTE ARMFIELD B. displayed gallantry & devotion to duty. Placed on duty as control post at the junction of LONG-ACRE and NEW TRENCH. The two sentries nearest him were killed. LONG-ACRE & NEW TRENCH were both blown in. He did not leave his post until properly relieved. OPERATIONS. Enemy artillery very active during the night, several shells dropping on front and support lines, also around Battalion Headqrs. Our Lewis Guns fired intermittently during the night on enemy wire. CASUALTIES. One man wounded. CAPTAIN. R.L. ILLINGWORTH, 2nd LIEUT. A. SCRAGG, and 2nd LIEUT A.L. HOLLAND attached to 16th RIFLE BRIGADE.	
	10th		OPERATIONS. Enemy exceptionally quiet during the day and night. In the evening considerable movement of transport was heard along STATION ROAD opposite our front line. Our batteries opened fire & dispersed the enemy. 2nd LIEUT. C. PARKS & 2nd LIEUT A.E. COOLING joined the Battalion for duty.	

Army Form C. 2118.

WAR DIARY
or
INTELLIGENCE SUMMARY.

No. 3

16TH (SER) BATT^N. SHERWOOD FORESTERS
(CHATSWORTH RIFLES)

Place	Date	Hour	Summary of Events and Information	Remarks and references to Appendices
BEAUMONT HAMEL.	SEPT 6TH 1916.		The Battalion moved into the trenches relieving the 4th GLOUCESTER REGT. 144th BRIGADE in the LONG-ACRE SECTOR BEAUMONT-HAMEL.	
	7TH.		OPERATIONS. NIL. CASUALTIES. 2. men wounded.	
	8TH.		RECOMMENDATIONS. Copy of Letter to G.O.C. 117TH BRIGADE. I beg to bring to your notice for favourable consideration the services of the following, during the Operations of 3-9-1916. No 26953. PTE ANNABLE J. acting as orderly to the Commanding Officer. He carried messages to and from carrying parties speedily and successfully under heavy shell fire and under circumstances of great difficulty, several of our trenches being obliterated by hostile shell fire. This man had previously taken part in two raids carried out by the Battalion and displayed marked gallantry, notably, when he carried a wounded man across "NO MAN'S LAND" under heavy fire on which occasion he was wounded. This man was again hit and killed when on ANNABLE'S task. No 10688. P^{te} ASTLE A. was one of a carrying party taking bombs from FORT. JACKSON to forward dump in BMD S^t. He took charge of the party when	

Army Form C. 2118.

WAR DIARY
or
INTELLIGENCE SUMMARY.

No. 5

18TH (SER) BATTN. SHERWOOD FORESTERS (CHATSWORTH RIFLES).

(Erase heading not required.)

Instructions regarding War Diaries and Intelligence Summaries are contained in F.S. Regs., Part II. and the Staff Manual respectively. Title pages will be prepared in manuscript.

Place	Date	Hour	Summary of Events and Information	Remarks and references to Appendices
BEAUMONT HAMEL	SEPT. 10TH 1916.		Draft of 100 men arrived from Base.	
	11TH		OPERATIONS. The enemy shelled our trenches intermittently during the day NORTH of the ANCRE with 4.2, and 77 shells and trench mortars. A large proportion of the shells were duds. Our Lewis Guns played on the enemies wire during the night, but they only retaliated with a few rifle shots. CASUALTIES. 5 men accidently wounded.	
	12TH		OPERATIONS. Enemy lightly shelled our trenches during the day and night, a few dropping on UXBRIDGE ROAD & SOUTH ALLEY, destroying a traverse. 2nd LIEUTENANTS. A.R. BUTLER, C.W. LAWS, E.J.H. BOWLER and V. BOWMER joined for duty. CASUALTIES. One man wounded.	
	13TH		2nd LIEUT. A. BAYZAND joined the Battalion for duty. Battalion relieved by the 17TH Battalion SHERWOOD FORESTERS in the LONG-ACRE SECTOR BEAUMONT-HAMEL and proceeded to Billets in MAILLY WOOD.	
	14TH		2nd LIEUT. A. STEVENSON granted special leave.	

Army Form C. 2118.

WAR DIARY
or
INTELLIGENCE SUMMARY.
(Erase heading not required.)

16TH (SER) BATTN. SHERWOOD FORESTERS (CHATSWORTH RIFLES).

Instructions regarding War Diaries and Intelligence Summaries are contained in F.S. Regs., Part II. and the Staff Manual respectively. Title pages will be prepared in manuscript.

No. 6.

Place	Date	Hour	Summary of Events and Information	Remarks and references to Appendices
MAILLY WOOD	Sept 10th 1916.		The enemy shelled VITERMONT close to MAILLY WOOD wounding one of our men on duty at 117TH INFANTRY BRIGADE HEADQUARTERS. A Football Match took place between our Officers, including the Commanding Officer and the Officers of the 252nd Coy. R.E.'s at MAILLY WOOD our side losing. The result was 2 goals to none. CAPTAIN J. G. COOKE granted Special leave. A.P.H. le PREVOST temporarily attached to 17TH BATTN SHERWOOD FORESTERS. LIEUT R.H. ELLIS appointed temporarily acting Regimental Transport Officer vice LIEUT. M. JACKSON to ENGLAND sick, with effect from SEPT 9TH 1916.	
	17TH		2ND LIEUT A.H. STRUTT promoted LIEUTENANT with effect from JULY 20TH/16 vice LIEUT. H.R. STEVENS transferred to General List for duty with Trench Mortal Batty. Provisionally appointed under Authority of 39TH DIVN pending publication of LONDON GAZETTE. 2ND LIEUT. C.I. HART promoted LIEUTENANT with effect from AUG. 22ND/16, vice LIEUT R.F. DUNN to ENGLAND AUG 21ST/16. Provisionally appointed under Authority of 39TH DIVISION pending publication of LONDON GAZETTE. The New Draft of 150 men were inspected Mr. G.O.C. after Church Parade.	

Army Form C. 2118.

WAR DIARY
or
INTELLIGENCE SUMMARY.

No. 2.   16TH (SER) BATTN. SHERWOOD FORESTERS
(CHATSWORTH RIFLES)

Place	Date	Hour	Summary of Events and Information	Remarks and references to Appendices
MAILLY WOOD	SEPT. 18TH 1916		2nd LIEUT. J.W. HASTINGS rejoined the Battalion after being wounded.	
	19TH	"	The Battalion marched from MAILLY WOOD and took over billets for the night at BERTRANCOURT.	
	20TH	"	The Battalion marched from BERTRANCOURT and relieved the 1st Battalion KINGS ROYAL RIFLES (2ND DIVISION) in the trenches on the RIGHT HEBUTERNE SECTION.	
HEBUTERNE	21ST	"	OPERATIONS. The enemy sent over a few trench mortars, otherwise operations were at a standstill. CASUALTIES. Nil.	
	22ND	"	OPERATIONS. Between 8 a.m. and 11 a.m. the enemy shelled our trenches around KNOX ST. & JONES ST. with trench mortars and rifle grenades, damaging the trenches in a few places which was quickly repaired. They also sent over a few 5.9 shells which caused little damage. Enemy Aeroplanes were very active during the day. CASUALTIES. One man wounded.	
	23RD		OPERATIONS. There was considerable aerial activity during the day, on both sides, the enemy reconnoitring our trenches and flying very low.	

Army Form C. 2118.

WAR DIARY
or
INTELLIGENCE SUMMARY.

N°. 8.

16TH (SER) BATTN. SHERWOOD FORESTER
(CHATSWORTH RIFLES).

(Erase heading not required.)

Place	Date	Hour	Summary of Events and Information	Remarks and references to Appendices
HEBUTERNE.	23rd 1916.		OPERATIONS. The enemy Put a good deal of shrapnel over, bursting around NAIRNE & JONES S'S causing a few casualties, otherwise operations were very quiet. CASUALTIES. 2nd LIEUT. A.R.BUTLER Wounded (at duty) and 2 men Wounded.	
	24TH		OPERATIONS. The enemy were very active during the day with rifle grenades, sending over about 30 during the afternoon, causing a slight casualty, and damaging a machine gun. A short bombardment of the enemy lui-toot place at 8.30 & 10 pm, the enemy retaliated with about 30 Trench Mortars which fell around JUNCTION of JONES & WRANGLE S'S, causing slight damage to the trenches. About 1 am Our Artillery dispersed a hostile Working Party. CASUALTIES. One man SHELL SHOCK. 2nd LIEUT. A. STEVENSON returned from ENGLAND on leave.	
	25TH		OPERATIONS. The enemy artillery very active during the day, sending over a good number of .77's on our left Coy Front. We retaliated with trench Mortars. In the afternoon the enemy sent over a few T.M's damaging the trenches in JONES S'T, NAIRNE S'T, JEAN BART, & FORE S'T, also causing a few casualties.	

Army Form C. 2118.

WAR DIARY or INTELLIGENCE SUMMARY.

(Erase heading not required.)

16TH (SER) BATTN. SHERWOOD FORESTER (CHATSWORTH RIFLES).

No. 9.

Place	Date	Hour	Summary of Events and Information	Remarks and references to Appendices
HEBUTERNE	Sept 25th 1916.		OPERATIONS Cont. Our Lewis Guns were very active during the night, dispersing two enemy working parties. CASUALTIES. One man killed, 2 men wounded.	
	26th		OPERATIONS. At 6 a.m. and 12 noon the enemy sent over a number of rifle grenades and minenwerfers, we retaliated effectively with Trench Mortars. In the afternoon they sent over about 40 large shells & a few minenwerfers in reply to our bombardment. We again bombarded the enemy trenches at 8.30 & 10 p.m. they replied with "77"s & minenwerfers which fell around PERE ST., KNOX ST & JEAN BART. CASUALTIES. One man wounded. A raid was carried out last night by the 1st Battalion KINGS ROYAL RIFLES CORPS. The party left our front line trenches at 10 p.m., they failed to reach the enemy trenches owing to new wire lying having been put out near the parapet of their own trenches to cover the gaps made in their wire. 2nd LIEUT. J.P. TEAHAN. joined the Battalion for duty.	
	27th			

Army Form C. 2118.

WAR DIARY
or
INTELLIGENCE SUMMARY.

(Erase heading not required.)

16TH (SER) BATTN. SHERWOOD FORESTERS
(CHATSWORTH RIFLES)

No. 10.

Place	Date	Hour	Summary of Events and Information	Remarks and references to Appendices
HEBUTERNE	SEP. 27TH 1916.		OPERATIONS. Until our bombardment commenced the situation was very quiet. To this the enemy replied with 5.9's and Trench Mortars on our LEFT Coy Headquarters, also around FORE ST, KNOX ST, & JONES where they damaged two fire bays, burying 5 men who were safely got out by a clearing party, two of these suffering from shock. CASUALTIES. 2 men wounded. CAPTAIN J. G. COOKE returned from ENGLAND from Special leave.	
	28TH		OPERATIONS. From 8 to 9.20 a.m. the enemy sent over a great number of 77 shells, about 20 falling just behind Battalion Headqrs, the remainder falling around KNOX St. & JEAN BART. Our artillery opened fire in cooperation with our Trench Mortars and apparently silencing the enemy. CASUALTIES. NIL. CAPTAIN A. HARDY assumed command of "O" Company. 2ND LIEUT. V. J. COPESTAKE joined the Battalion for duty.	
	29TH			

Army Form C. 2118.

WAR DIARY
or
INTELLIGENCE SUMMARY.
(Erase heading not required.)

16TH (SER) BATTN SHERWOOD FORESTERS
(CHATSWORTH RIFLES).

No. 11.

Place	Date	Hour	Summary of Events and Information	Remarks and references to Appendices
HEBUTERNE.	SEPT 29TH	1916.	DECORATIONS. The Commanding Officer has much pleasure in notifying under authority of the General Officer Commanding-in-Chief that the undermentioned N.C.O.s & men have been awarded the following decoration:- No. 26230. H/Sgt. HOLYWELL. C.E. ⎫ 10668. Pte. ASTLE A. ⎬ MILITARY MEDAL. 26593. " ANNABLE J. ⎭ The Commanding Officer feels sure that all ranks will join with him in congratulating most heartily the recipients. OPERATIONS. A rather more lively day. Between 6 a.m & 12 noon the enemy sent over a number of rifle grenades, 7.7's & L.2's, falling around our left Coy front, and apparently searching for our Trench Mortars. We retaliated, and they again replied with rifle 5.9's, 4.2's, & 7.7's. Trench Mortars & grenades falling around JONES S! We brought a German Aeroplane down behind their own lines at 4.30 p.m.	
	30TH		OPERATIONS. The enemy were much quieter during the day and only sent out a few rifle grenades & T.M. Our machine guns were very active on enemy wire.	

Chas Vessey LIEUT. COLONEL.
Commanding 16th SERVICE Bn. SHERWOOD FORESTERS,
(CHATSWORTH RIFLES)

117th Brigade.
39th Division.
----------- ---

1/16th BATTALION

NOTTS & DERBY REGIMENT

OCTOBER 1916

Army Form C. 2118.

WAR DIARY or INTELLIGENCE SUMMARY.

16TH (SER) BATTN. SHERWOOD FORESTERS. (CHATSWORTH RIFLES).

No. 1.

Place	Date	Hour	Summary of Events and Information	Remarks and references to Appendices
HEBUTERNE	10.16 Oct 1st		The Battalion was relieved in the HEBUTERNE SECTOR by the 13TH BATTN ESSEX REGIMENT and proceeded to Billets at BERTRANCOURT. CASUALTIES. One man shell shock.	
BERTRANCOURT	" 3rd		The Battalion marched from BERTRANCOURT to Billets in MARTINSART-WOOD and came under the orders of the 2nd CORPS commanded.	
MARTINSART WOOD	" 5th		The 117TH BRIGADE relieved the 53rd INFANTRY BRIGADE of the 18TH DIVISION on the battlefield in the THIEPVAL SECTOR. The Battalion took over the CENTRE SECTOR from the 7TH BATTALION BUFFS excluding SCHWABEN REDOUBT with Headquarters at THIEPVAL CHATEAU. The relief was carried out by daylight and the Battalion came in for heavy shelling. CASUALTIES. One man killed, one man missing, 26 men wounded. CASUALTIES. 2nd LIEUT. A.R. BUTLER wounded.	
THIEPVAL	" 6th " 7th		The enemy made a determined attack on the SCHWABEN REDOUBT, at the same time putting a heavy barrage on THIEPVAL and also using	

WAR DIARY
or
INTELLIGENCE SUMMARY.

Army Form C. 2118.

16TH (SER) BATTN. SHERWOOD FORESTERS.
(CHATSWORTH RIFLES).

No. 2.

Place	Date	Hour	Summary of Events and Information	Remarks and references to Appendices
MIRAUMONT	1916 Oct. 7th		Flammenwerfer. The enemy were successfully driven back by the 16th and 17th BATTALIONS SHERWOOD FORESTERS with heavy enemy losses and also leaving a number of prisoners in our hands. The following letter was received from the II CORPS COMMANDER:— "The CORPS COMMANDER wishes to express to the 16th & 17th BATTALIONS SHERWOOD FORESTERS his congratulations on their action in dealing with the GERMAN COUNTER ATTACKS on the evening of the 7th and morning of the 8th OCTOBER, the results of which are so complimentary to units concerned as they must be discouraging to the enemy." The following letter was received from G.O.C. 117th INFANTRY BRIGADE on the Operations of October 7th and 8th:— "I think the work carried out by the 16th & 17th SHERWOOD FORESTERS was very satisfactory. All worked coolly and methodically, their supported each other, liason with Artillery was very complete and satisfactory and all units showed much spirit and dash"	
	Oct. 9th		In accordance with orders, the Battalion made an attack on the	

Army Form C. 2118.

WAR DIARY
or
INTELLIGENCE SUMMARY.
(Erase heading not required.)

16TH (SER) BATTN. SHERWOOD FORESTERS (CHATSWORTH RIFLES).

No. 3.

Instructions regarding War Diaries and Intelligence Summaries are contained in F. S. Regs., Part II. and the Staff Manual respectively. Title pages will be prepared in manuscript.

Place	Date	Hour	Summary of Events and Information	Remarks and references to Appendices
THIEPVAL	1916. 04.9.17		SCHWABEN REDOUBT at 4-30.a.m. The point to be attacked were:— "B" COMPANY. POINT 99. "C" " " 69 to 119. "D" " " 39. "A" " " Obten. There was a artillery preparation. In the early morning the assault was successfully carried out in spite of heavy shelling. The Companies started in depth. The assault was carried out at 4-30.a.m under cover of darkness, the assaulting waves had not gone more than half the distance across NO MAN'S LAND before enemy machine guns and rifle fire was opened. The enemy barrage was not put on until 4-38.a.m, although there was some intermittent shelling. "B" COMPANY succeeded in reaching its objective and passing between Points 99 & 69 made good the German Trench, but in so doing they received a large number of casualties. "C" COMPANY on arriving at the front line of the German trenches	

WAR DIARY
or
INTELLIGENCE SUMMARY.
(Erase heading not required.)

Army Form C. 2118.

16TH (SER) BATTN. SHERWOOD FORESTERS
(CHATSWORTH RIFLES).

No. 4.

Place	Date	Hour	Summary of Events and Information	Remarks and references to Appendices
THIEPVAL	1916. Oct. 7th		found there was a considerable amount of wire in front. "D" COMPANY was held up just SOUTH OF POINT 39, with heavy machine gun and rifle fire. The fight lasted about 2 hours when our bombs were exhausted. "B" COMPANY was assisted in the operation by one platoon of the 17th BATTN SHERWOOD FORESTERS. The enemy eventually forced the party back and POINT 99 was lost. A large number of Germans were killed, especially about 9.99 where enemy dug-outs were bombed. Our casualties were heavy numbering 13 Officers as under:- LIEUT. C. J. HART. KILLED 2nd " L. W. GODWIN. " 2nd " A. BAYZAND. " CAPTAIN J. G. COOKE. MISSING 2nd LIEUT. J. P. TEAHAN. " CAPTAIN A. HARDY. WOUNDED LIEUT. P. U. LAWS. " LIEUT. W. R. A. LEHMANDT. DIED OF WOUNDS 2nd " A. SCRAGG WOUNDED 2nd " A. E. COOLING " 2nd " E. DARKE " 2nd " G. W. LAWS " 2nd " H. Y. COPESTAKE " Other Ranks 26 Killed, 134 Wounded & 64 missing including No 05552 C.S.M. LILLIMAN, Killed and No 6366 C.S.M. MILLER Wounded	

Army Form C. 2118.

WAR DIARY
or
INTELLIGENCE SUMMARY.

(Erase heading not required.)

16TH (SER) BATTN. SHERWOOD FORESTERS.
(CHATSWORTH RIFLES).

No. 5

Place	Date	Hour	Summary of Events and Information	Remarks and references to Appendices
THIEPVAL	1916 Oct. 9TH	1. P.M.	The Battalion was relieved by the 17th Battalion Kings Royal Rifle Corps and proceeded to Reserve Line Wood Post, AUTHILLE. CAPTAIN R.L. ILLINGWORTH Rejoined the Battalion from 10TH BN R.B. BRIGADE. 2ND LIEUT. A.L. HOLLAND. " "	
	10TH		The Battalion was relieved by the 1/1ST CAMBRIDGE REGT, and proceeded to Billets at SENLIS	
SENLIS	11TH		MAJOR W.G. CONSTABLE, acting SECOND IN COMMAND transferred to 11TH BN. LANCASHIRE FUSILIERS.	
	12TH		MAJOR. N. HOUGHTON. proceeded to ENGLAND on sick leave.	
	14TH		2. Officers and 100 other ranks sent to assist the 118TH INFANTRY BRIGADE as additional stretcher bearers during their attack on the remainder of SCHWABEN REDOUBT. SCHWABEN REDOUBT was subsequently taken by 2 Battalions of the 118TH BRIGADE namely 4/5TH BLACK WATCH & 4 CAMBRIDGES, assisted by 2 Companies of the 17TH BN K.R.R. CORPS. and a heavy artillery barrage.	
	16TH		The Battalion relieved the 16TH CHESHIRE REGT. in the LEFT RIVER ANCRE SECTOR.	

Army Form C. 2118.

WAR DIARY
or
INTELLIGENCE SUMMARY.

16TH (SER) BATTN. SHERWOOD FORESTERS
(CHATSWORTH RIFLES).

No. 6.

Place	Date	Hour	Summary of Events and Information	Remarks and references to Appendices
THIEPVAL RIVER ANCRE SECTOR	1916 Oct. 17th - 18th		CASUALTIES. 2 men killed.	
	20th		CASUALTIES. 1 man wounded. 2nd LIEUT. E.S. ESAM joined the Battalion for duty. CASUALTIES. one man wounded, one man gas poisoning.	
	21st		CAPTAIN. L.H. ASKWITH ⎫ LIEUT. S.G. BURCH ⎬ Joined the Battalion for duty. " F.P. HOLMES ⎭	
	22nd		2nd LIEUT. A. STEVENSON granted special leave to England.	
	24th		CAPTAIN. H.R. STEVENS of this Battalion, COMDG. 117th LIGHT TRENCH MORTAR BATTERY, awarded the "MILITARY CROSS".	
	25th		The Battalion was relieved by the 1st CAMBRIDGE REGT. in the RIVER ANCRE SECTOR and proceeded to BILLETS at PIONEER ROAD.	
	26th		LIEUT. R. URE joined the Battalion for duty	

Army Form C. 2118.

WAR DIARY
or
INTELLIGENCE SUMMARY.
(Erase heading not required.)

10TH (SER) BATTN. SHERWOOD FORESTERS.
(CHATSWORTH RIFLES.)

N° 7.

Place	Date	Hour	Summary of Events and Information	Remarks and references to Appendices
PIONEER ROAD.	1916 OCT 26TH		LIEUT. T.L. DARBYSHIRE } Joined the Battalion for duty 2nd " P.J. DUNCKLEY }	
THIEPVAL	27TH		LIEUT. E.E. BULL Joined the Battalion for duty as Transport Officer. The Battalion relieved the 11TH BATTN HANTS REGT. (116TH BRIGADE) in the RIVER SECTOR THIEPVAL & became Battalion in BRIGADE SUPPORT with Headquarters at THIEPVAL CHATEAU	
	28TH		The Commanding Officer has much pleasure in notifying under authority of the General Officer Commanding-in-Chief that the undermentioned Officers and N.C.Os have been awarded the following decorations:— CAPTAIN. P.H. COLERIDGE. } 2nd LIEUT. A. STEVENSON. } THE MILITARY CROSS REV. A.P. DANIELS } N° 26965. 4/SGT. H. HALLAM. THE DISTINGUISHED CONDUCT MEDAL. 26156. SGT. P. TRUEMAN. THE MILITARY MEDAL. The Commanding Officer feels sure that all ranks will join with him in congratulating most heartily the recipients.	

WAR DIARY
INTELLIGENCE SUMMARY

16TH (SER) BATTN. SHERWOOD FORESTERS (CHATSWORTH RIFLES)

No. 8

Army Form C. 2118.

Place	Date	Hour	Summary of Events and Information	Remarks and references to Appendices
MARTINSART WOOD	1916 Oct. 29TH		The Battalion was relieved in the RIVER SECTOR THIEPVAL by the 11th CAMBRIDGE REGT and proceeded to Billets in MARTINSART WOOD.	
	31ST		LIEUT. C. G. LORD promoted CAPTAIN. with effect from 12-10-16.	

Charles Shepley
LIEUT. COLONEL
COMMANDING 16th SERVICE Bn. SHERWOOD FORESTERS,
(CHATSWORTH RIFLES).

117th Brigade.
39th Division.

1/16th BATTALION

NOTTS & DERBY REGIMENT

NOVEMBER 1 9 1 6

WAR DIARY or INTELLIGENCE SUMMARY

Army Form C. 2118

11th (Service) Battalion Sherwood Foresters (Chatsworth Rifles)

39/117

Vol 9

9.A.

Place	Date	Hour	Summary of Events and Information	Remarks and references to Appendices
Martinsart Wood	Nov. 2/10		The Battalion came out of the Line.	
Paisley Dump	Nov. 3rd		Proceeded from MARTINSART WOOD to PAISLEY DUMP, LEFT RIVER ANCRE SECTION, relieving 4/5th Black Watch.	
	Nov. 5th.		The Battalion was relieved by 11th Bn. Sussex Regt. and proceeded to Billets at SENLIS.	
SENLIS	Nov. 6th		2nd Lt. C.L. GARLAND proceeded on special leave to ENGLAND. The Battalion proceeded from SENLIS to PAISLEY DUMP, LEFT RIVER ANCRE SECTION, and relieved the 11th Bn. Sussex Regt.	
PAISLEY DUMP	Nov. 7th		2nd Lt. R.A. JOHNSON joined the Battalion for duty. Draft of 38 men arrived from Base.	
SOUTH BLUFF	Nov. 8th		Relieved by 1st Battn. HERTS REGT. and proceed to SOUTH BLUFF in reserve.	
	Nov. 9th		2nd Lt. T. WILLIAMS and 2nd Lt. A.S. MELLOR joined the Battalion for duty.	
MARTINSART WOOD	Nov. 11th		Battalion proceeded from SOUTH BLUFF to MARTINS RT WOODS. Draft of 50 men arrived from Base.	
	Nov. 12th		According to orders the Battalion marched from MARTINSART WOOD to the LEFT RIVER ANCRE SECTION.	

CAPTURE of St. PIERRE DIVION.

On November 13th the Battalion was ordered to make a subsidiary attack from the South up the RIVER ANCRE in conjunction with a main attack by the 118th Infantry Brigade. The objective of the Battalion was a line running East from the SUMMER HOUSE and short of St. PIERRE DIVION.

The 4/5th Black Watch were to join up with us from the East.
The 1/6th Cheshire Regt. were to capture St. PIERRE DIVION.
The main attack was to start at 5.45 a.m.
The 16th Sherwoods were to advance with three Companies at 6.13 a.m., one Company being left in reserve.
A Tank was to co-operate on our right.
The assembly was successfully carried out without incident and the troops advanced at the

WAR DIARY
or
INTELLIGENCE SUMMARY

(Erase heading not required.)

Army Form C. 2118

Place	Date	Hour	Summary of Events and Information	Remarks and references to Appendices
			Capture of St. PIERRE DIVION continued.....	

scheduled time in a thick mist.

The Battalion successfully entered the German First Line trench, but here met with a certain amount of opposition and the right was held up.

At 6.30 a.m. the reserve Company was sent up to reinforce the right. Their arrival helped to clear the situation and the Battalion advanced bombing & driving the enemy before them into their dugouts.

The objective allotted to the Battalion was secured but nothing could stop our men, who advanced with the greatest dash and finally secured the whole of St. PIERRE DIVION including the German Battalion Headquarters and the famous tunnel dugouts.

A party under 2nd Lieut. A.L. HOLLAND continued their advance as far as the HANSA LINE joining up with the 1/1st HERTS REGT on the extreme right of the 118th Brigade.

At 8.15 a.m. owing to our running short of bombs and to so many men being required to guard the entrances of dugouts and guard prisoners, a Company of the 17th Sherwood Foresters were sent up to this Company and rendered most useful assistance.

By 9 o'clock however the whole position was in our hands and there remained only to clear the dugouts of prisoners.

At 9.15 a.m. Battalion Headquarters moved forward to the German Battalion Headquarters taking with them two more Companies of the 17th Battalion Sherwood Foresters to consolidate the line.

13 Officers including the Battalion Commander and 720 Other Ranks were taken prisoners.

Our casualties were slight and consisted of :-
    Lieut. S.G.BURCH   } Killed
    4 Other Ranks   }
    67 Other Ranks including Company Sergeant Major J.H.Robinson wounded.

The 1/1st HERTS REGT.
The 4/5th BLACK WATCH. lost direction to the right and took no part in the capture of the fortress.

The 4/5th BLACK WATCH lost direction in the mist and only two Officers and 10 men arrived at their objective. This party rendered us useful assistance.

The Tank arrived at the German Front Line before its scheduled time and unfortunately subsided into a dugout and was put out of action.

Army Form C. 2118

WAR DIARY
or
INTELLIGENCE SUMMARY
(Erase heading not required.)

Instructions regarding War Diaries and Intelligence Summaries are contained in F.S. Regs., Part II. and the Staff Manual respectively. Title Pages will be prepared in manuscript.

Place	Date	Hour	Summary of Events and Information	Remarks and references to Appendices
PAISLEY AVENUE			Many fine feats were performed by the Battalion notably by:— Captain R.L. ILLINGWORTH who with only his orderly entered the famous tunnel dugout and brought out 81 Germans. It was necessary to advance 150 yards down this deep tunnel to reach the dug out where the enemy had taken refuge. 2nd Lieut. HOLLAND who advanced with great dash and secured the German Battalion Headquarters and took prisoner the German Battalion Commander and 60 Other Ranks. Sergt. Cook Cpl. Monks who despite his 56 years entered a defended dugout single handed and brought out 6 prisoners. Many other Officers, N.C.O's and men performed feats of exceptional gallantry which have been brought to the notice of Higher Authority. White Star bombs (poison gas) were used for the first time and were found most effective in dealing with dugouts from which the enemy had been sniping or bombing. At 9.30 a.m. we started to dig in a new line and to consolidate the position. A large amount of booty fell into our hands but it was not possible to enumerate it. The Battalion was relieved at 7.15 p.m. and proceeded to PAISLEY AVENUE. It may be stated that the 4 assaulting Companies attacked each about 90 strong. The fire was admirably cut by our artillery, and the barrage of the 85 h Battery, 18th Division was beyond all praise.	
	Nov 14th		The Battalion was relieved by the 15th Battalion Lancashire Fusiliers, and then proceeded to camp at HARLOV under canvas, during the night enemy aircraft (owing to a bright moon) succeeded in dropping six bombs on the camp wounding a mule, otherwise no serious damage was done. CASUALTIES:- One man accidentally wounded. Copy of letter received by Major-General G.J.CUTHBERT. C.B. C.M.G. Commanding 39th Division "Your Division is now leaving the 2nd Corps and I wish to thank you all for the excellent work you have done since you came into the Corps and took over the line at the SCHWABEN REDOUBT and down to the RIVER ANCRE. You have had a good deal of hard fighting which has shewn up the good qualities of your Brigades and Battalions and the spirit and dash of the men has been most conspicuous. We shall always remember the gallant defence of the SCHWABEN REDOUBT and the way your troops beat off counter attack after counter attack.	

Army Form C. 2118

WAR DIARY
or
INTELLIGENCE SUMMARY

(Erase heading not required.)

Instructions regarding War Diaries and Intelligence Summaries are contained in F.S. Regs., Part II. and the Staff Manual respectively. Title Pages will be prepared in manuscript.

Place	Date	Hour	Summary of Events and Information	Remarks and references to Appendices
			The capture of St. PIERRE DIVION and the HANSA line on the 13th inst. was a splendid feat and a very fitting conclusion to the operations of your Division before leaving the 2nd. Corps. The results of that capture will be far reaching, not only on account of the number of prisoners and material you took, but on account of the assistance you gave to the 5th Corps and the damaging effect on the moral of the enemy. Will you please tell your Brigade Commanders, Battalion and Company Commanders and all ranks in the Division that their work all through has been thoroughly appreciated and that the departure of the Division is much regretted. Success in war cannot be obtained unless all arms co-operate and work together in close combination. The many successes your Division has had is due to the untiring support you have had from the artillery, which has never failed you. The calls on the Divisional Artillery have been heavy, but their response has always been prompt and efficient. Will you kindly convey to the C.R.A. of the 18th and 39th Divisional Artilleries the thanks of the 2nd Corps for the efficient way all ranks of the gunners have "played the game". (signed) C.W. JACOB Lt. General Commanding IInd Corps. G. 4280. Nov. 15. Copy of telegram received from IInd Corps. Following message received from First Army begins. The following gracious telegram has been received from His Majesty the King to the address of GENERAL SIR DOUGLAS HAIG begins. I heartily congratulate you upon the great success achieved by my gallant troops during the past three days in the advance on both sides of the ANCRE. This further capture of the enemy's first line trenches under special difficulties owing to the recent wet weather redounds to the credit of all ranks. Ends:- Please communicate to all ranks.	
WARLOY	NOV. 15		The Battalion marched from WARLOY and was billetted in GEZAINCOURT near DOULLENS en route for the North.	
GEZAIN- COURT	NOV. 17	5.30 a.m.	The Battalion proceeded to CANDAS and entrained for the NORTH arriving at ESQUELBECQ at morning of the 18th, afterwards marching to VOLKERINCKHOVE and took over billets.	

Army Form C. 2118

WAR DIARY
or
INTELLIGENCE SUMMARY
(Erase heading not required.)

Instructions regarding War Diaries and Intelligence Summaries are contained in F. S. Regs., Part II. and the Staff Manual respectively. Title Pages will be prepared in manuscript.

Place	Date	Hour	Summary of Events and Information	Remarks and references to Appendices
VOLAERINCK- HOVE.	NOV. 18th		The Battalion came under orders of the 2nd Army, commanded by General Sir HERBERT C. O. PLUMER G.C.M.G. K.C.B.	
	NOV. 21st		The Battalion was inspected by Brigadier General R.D.F. OLDMAN D.S.O at VOLMERINCKHOVE who congratulated the Battalion on the capture of St. PIERRE DIVION.	
	NOV. 21st.		Captain S. F. Lilley assumed command of the Battalion during the temporary absence of Lieut. Colonel C. Herbert Stepney, who took over the command of the 117th Infantry Brigade during the absence on leave in England of Brigadier General R.D.F. OLDMAN D.S.O. On November 21st the Battalion was inspected by Lieut. General Sir AYLMER HUNTER WESTON K.C.B. D.S.O. Commanding VIIIth ARMY CORPS, who congratulated the Commanding Officer on the smart turn out and bearing of all ranks.	
	NOV. 22nd		Capt. F. H. COLERIDGE proceeded on leave to ENGLAND.	
	NOV. 23rd		Capt. S. J. L. LINDMAN (Medical Officer) proceeded on leave to England. Lieut. A. J. BADO took over Medical charge of the Battalion.	
	NOV. 26th		2nd Lieut. V. J. COPESTAKE – awarded MILITARY CROSS for gallantry in the attack on SCHWABEN REDOUBT on October 9th 1916.	
	NOV. 29th		Capt. R. L. IVINGWORTH and 2nd Lieut. A. L. HOLLAND proceeded on leave to England.	

LIEUT. COLONEL,
COMMANDING 16th SERVICE Bn. SHERWOOD FORESTERS,
(CHATSWORTH RIFLES).

117th Brigade.
39th Division.

1/16th BATTALION

NOTTS & DERBY REGIMENT

DECEMBER 1 9 1 6

WAR DIARY or INTELLIGENCE SUMMARY

Army Form C. 2118.

16th Battalion Sherwood Foresters

Vol 10

Place	Date	Hour	Summary of Events and Information	Remarks and references to Appendices
WARINGHEM 1916	DEC 1st.		Lt. Colonel C. Herbert Stepney proceeded on leave to England.	
	DEC 4th.		Lieut. R. H. Ellis reported for duty to C.R.E. 4th Army.	
	DEC 5th.		Major M. Boughton rejoined Battalion and took over the command of the Battalion.	
	DEC 6th.		The Battalion was inspected in billets by Brigadier General R.D.F. OXMAN D.S.O.	
			The Battalion was inspected on the march by General Sir C.C. FLETCHER C.B.,K.C.M.G. V.C.B. who expressed his appreciation of the fine bearing and smart turn out of all ranks, and congratulated the Battalion on their fine fighting on the SOMME.	
			Captain S. F. Lilley proceeded on leave to England.	
	DEC 7th.		Captain R. H. Truscott rejoined the Battalion from Hunstial.	
	DEC 8th.		The Battalion was inspected by [Hon'] General Sir Arthur Hughes Wilton F.C.B. D.S.O. the congratulated the Commanding Officer on the splendid appearance of the men and turn out generally. He afterwards inspected the Transport and Officers Mess and the billets of "B" Company with which he expressed his satisfaction.	
			Captain S. J. L. Lindeman and 2n'd Lt. C. F. Garland rejoined the Battalion from leave.	
	DEC 10th		Major H. A. Leggett joined the Battalion.	
			Advance Party of 1 Officer and 8 Other Ranks and Lewis Gun teams left VOLKERINCKHOVE for POPERINGHE.	

Army Form C. 2118.

WAR DIARY
or
INTELLIGENCE SUMMARY
(Erase heading not required.)

16th ... Sherwood Foresters

Instructions regarding War Diaries and Intelligence Summaries are contained in F. S. Regs., Part II. and the Staff Manual respectively. Title Pages will be prepared in manuscript.

Place	Date	Hour	Summary of Events and Information	Remarks and references to Appendices
VOLKERINGHOVE	DEC 11th 1916		The Battalion proceeded by march route to BOLLEZELE STATION where the Battalion entrained for POPERINGHE. On arrival at POPERINGHE the Battalion was met by the advance party and took over billets for the night. Captain C. G. Lord proceeded on leave to England. Captain R. L. Illingworth and 2nd Lt. A. L. Keller rejoined the Battalion from leave.	
POPERINGHE	DEC 12th		No.22796 Pte. J. Betts awarded D.C.M. for gallant conduct during attack on SCHWABEN REDOUBT on 9/10/16. The Battalion entrained in the afternoon for POPERINGHE for YPRES. The same night taking over support billets of the centre sub-section YPRES SALIENT with Headquarters at CHATEAU des TROIS TOURS.	
YPRES	Dec 13th		The Battalion relieved the 13th Battalion Royal Welsh Fusiliers in the right sub-section YPRES SALIENT. The relief was carried out without incident. 2nd Lt. F. S. Esam attached to 117th Light Trench Mortar Battery.	
	DEC 15th		Lt. Colonel C. Herbert Stepney rejoined the Battalion from leave.	
	DEC 16th		Lt. Colonel C. Herbert Stepney proceeded on a course for Commanding Officers Officers at LOUVIE CHARM CHATEAU.	
	DEC 17th		The Battalion was relieved in the right sub-section YPRES SALIENT by the 17th Bn. King's Royal Rifle Corps, and went into Support with 2 Companies Headquarters at CHATEAU des TROIS TOURS and 2 Companies on CANAL BANK. 2nd Lts. W.H.Speechly and L.A.Gotland joined the Battalion.	

Army Form C. 2118.

10th Bn. Sherwood Foresters.

Instructions regarding War Diaries and Intelligence Summaries are contained in F. S. Regs., Part II. and the Staff Manual respectively. Title Pages will be prepared in manuscript.

WAR DIARY
or
INTELLIGENCE SUMMARY
(Erase heading not required.)

Place	Date	Hour	Summary of Events and Information	Remarks and references to Appendices
YPRES.	1916.			
	DEC 18th.		Captain L. B. Askwith rejoined the Battalion from Hospital.	
			Lieut. P. E. Burrows joined the Battalion	
	DEC 19th		Captain S. F. Lilley rejoined the Battalion from leave.	
	DEC 20th		The Billets of the Battalion were inspected by Brigadier General R.D.F.OLDMAN D.S.O. Commanding 117th Infantry Brigade.	
			Captain P. T. Coleridge M.C. rejoined the Battalion from leave.	
			2nd Lt. W. A. Medcalf joined the Battalion	
	DEC 21st.		The Battalion relieved the 17th Battalion King's Royal Rifle Corps in the right sub-section YPRES SALIENT.	
	DEC 22nd		A quiet day.	
	DEC 23rd		Enemy bombarded our front & support trench line with M.F., Minnenwerfer & Shrapnel causing... Casualties 2 killed, 13 wounded.	
			Captain C. G. Lord returned from leave.	
			Captain R. F. Truscott proceeded on leave to England.	
			No. 22796 Pte. Butts J. awarded the SILVER MEDAL for BRAVERY by His Majesty the King of Montenegro	
	DEC 24th.		Lt. Colonel C. Herbert Sturdy rejoined the Battalion from Course at LOUVI CRANK CHATEAU Between 2 & 3 p.m. our artillery bombarded enemy trenches with good effect. His draw was on retaliation.	
			CASUALTIES: Other Rank 3 Killed, 7 wounded.	
	DEC 25th		The Battalion was relieved by the 17th Battn. "King" Royal Rifle Corps and took over the Support Billets on CANAL BANKS & CHATEAU des TROIS TOURS.	

Army Form C. 2118.

10th Bn. Sherwood Foresters

WAR DIARY
or
INTELLIGENCE SUMMARY

(Erase heading not required.)

Instructions regarding War Diaries and Intelligence Summaries are contained in F. S. Regs., Part II. and the Staff Manual respectively. Title Pages will be prepared in manuscript.

Place	Date	Hour	Summary of Events and Information	Remarks and references to Appendices
YPRES.	1916. DEC 28th		2nd Lt. C. F. Bower proceeded on leave to England.	
	DEC 29th		2nd Lts. B. T. McPherson, N.P.Wright, H.M.Meakin joined the Battalion. The Ba'tn relieved the 17th King's Royal Rifle Corps in the right sub-section YPRES SALIENT.	
	DEC. 30th		Major F. A. Leggett appointed Commander 30th Divisional Mussastry School. Lt. Colonel C. Herbert Stepney proceeded to WISQUES near St. OMER on Course of 2nd Army Infantry School. Major N. Houlton assumed command of the Battalion during the absence of Lieut. Colonel C. Herbert Stepney.	
	DEC. 31st.		Extract from letter received by the Commanding Officer, from HIS GRACE THE DUKE of DEVONSHIRE K.G. GOVERNOR GENERAL of CANADA :- "Your letter of November 18th 1916 reached me here to-day (December 4th 1916) The Battalion has really done splendidly and I congratulate you all most sincerely. I hope you will say how pleased and proud we all are.	

N. Houlton Major
Comdg 10th Bn Sherwood Foresters

16th (Service) Battalion Sherwood Foresters.

WAR DIARY
or
INTELLIGENCE SUMMARY.

Army Form C. 2118.

Vol XI

Place	Date	Hour	Summary of Events and Information	Remarks and references to Appendices
YPRES	1917 JAN. 1st		The Battalion was relieved by 17th Battalion SHERWOOD FORESTERS, in the right sub-section, YPRES SALIENT, and took over the support billets on CANAL BANK and CHATEAU des TROIS TOURS.	
	JAN 2nd		2nd Lieutenant A. STEVENSON promoted CAPTAIN with effect from OCTOBER 31st, 1916.	
	JAN 3rd		NEW YEAR HONOURS:- Lieut Col. C. Herbert Stepney, mentioned in Despatches. Lieut P. U. Laws. Mentioned in Despatches. Lieut J. R. Chilterton, awarded M.C.	
	JAN 4th		Under authority of the Commander-in-Chief, the following decorations were awarded for gallantry in action on 13/11/1916 in the attack on ST. PIERRE DIVION. Lieut. Col. C. Herbert Stepney. D.S.O. Captain R. E. ILLINGWORTH. MILITARY CROSS. 2nd Lieut R. A. JOHNSON. " 2nd Lieut A. L. HOLLAND. " 2nd Lieut V. BOMMER. " Lt.D.W.STEVENS. MILITARY CROSS No. 26683 Sgt STYCH. S. A. D.C.M. 26777 " FREEMAN. E. D.C.M. 7659 " MONKS. C. MILITARY MEDAL. 25592 " WHITEHEAD. W. " 26208 L/S SHELDON. E. " 26563 Cpl JAYNES. E. " 26080 " BUSH. A. " 25592 " MITCHELL. A. " 27198 " RUSHTON. A. " 25748 L/C BARKES. T. W. " 26804 Pte. FARNATH. H. " 25375 " FOWKES. W. " 27620 " HOWITT. J. " 70079 " ROOT. W. " 27479 " EAKIN. W. " CASUALTIES..... 1 Other Rank. Wounded.	

WAR DIARY
or
INTELLIGENCE SUMMARY.
(Erase heading not required.)

Army Form C. 2118.

Instructions regarding War Diaries and Intelligence Summaries are contained in F.S. Regs., Part II. and the Staff Manual respectively. Title pages will be prepared in manuscript.

Place	Date	Hour	Summary of Events and Information	Remarks and references to Appendices
	JAN 4th		2nd Lieut T. C. C. WILLIAMS proceeded on leave to England.	
	JAN 5th		The Battalion relieved the 17th Battalion Sherwood Foresters in the right sub-section YPRES SALIENT 2nd Lieut V. BOWMER.) Wounded. C.S.M. AREINSTALL. W.)	
	JAN 7th		Lieut Colonel C. Herbert Stepney. D.S.O. rejoined the Battalion from a Course at WISQUES near ST. OMER.	
	JAN 8th		Captain R. F. TRUSCOTT, returned from leave of absence.	
YPRES SALIENT	JAN 9th		The Battalion was inspected in the trenches by Lieut General Sir Aylmer Hunter Weston, K.C.B., D.S.O. Commanding VIII Corps. The Battalion was relieved by the 17th Battalion Sherwood Foresters in the right sub-section YPRES SALIENT, and took over the support billets in CANAL BANK, and CHATEAU des TROIS TOURS. 2nd Lieut C. F. Bower returned from leave of absence. CASUALTIES... 1 Other Rank Wounded.	
	JAN 10th		2nd Lieut P. J. Dunckley proceeded to England to take up a Commission in the Indian Army Reserve of Officers. Enemy shelled CHATEAU des TROIS TOURS and in the vicinity. There were no casualties, and only very slight damage was done to the mens billets.	
	JAN 12th		The Battalion relieved the 17th Battalion Sherwood Foresters in the Right sub-Section, Centre Brigade. CASUALTIES... 2 wounded.	
	JAN 13th		The Xmas boxes kindly provided for all ranks of the Battalion by the people of Derbyshire, were distributed to the Battalion.	
BRANDHOEK.	JAN 14th		The Battalion was relieved by the 14th Battalion Royal Welsh Fusiliers, and proceeded to "B" Camp, near POPERINGHE. The day was marked by much hostile activity, EALING TRENCH being blown in, considerably delaying the inter-Battalion relief.	

Army Form C. 2118.

WAR DIARY
or
INTELLIGENCE SUMMARY.
(Erase heading not required.)

Instructions regarding War Diaries and Intelligence Summaries are contained in F.S. Regs., Part II. and the Staff Manual respectively. Title pages will be prepared in manuscript.

Place	Date	Hour	Summary of Events and Information	Remarks and references to Appendices
BRANDHOEK.	JAN. 16th.		The Battalion celebrated Xmas Day at "B" Camp, near POPERINGHE. Xmas fare was provided for all ranks of the Battalion.	
	JAN. 17th.		2nd Lieut J. H. Gosling proceeded on leave to England. A Concert was held in the CHURCH ARMY HUT near "B" Camp at which the majority of the Battalion were present. Pte HARRISON, "C" Company won the 2nd ARMY WELTER WEIGHT BOXING COMPETITION at WISQUES near ST. OMER.	
	JAN. 18th.		2nd Lieut T. C. O. WILLIAMS rejoined the Battalion from leave of absence.	
	JAN. 19th.		Captain S. J. L. LINDEMAN, R.A.M.C., Medical Officer to the Battalion, admitted to Field Ambulance. Lieut G. H. L. RIXON, assumed Medical charge of the Battalion.	
	JAN. 23rd.		GENERAL SIR HERBERT C. O. PLUMER. G.C.M.G. K.C.B. Commanding 2nd Army, inspected the Battalion whilst in training at "B" Camp near POPERINGHE. Draft of 57 Other Ranks joined the Battalion from Base. Captain C. G. LORD proceeded to 39th Divisional Reinforcement Camp as Company Commander. A Concert was held in the CHURCH ARMY HUT, near "B" Camp. Brigadier General R. D. F. OLDMAN, D.S.O., was present.	
YPRES.	JAN. 25th.		The Battalion relieved the 17th Battalion Sherwood Foresters on the CANAL BANK, KAAIE, and became LEFT SUPPORT BATTALION WIELTJE SECTION. Draft of 72 Other Ranks joined the Battalion. The weather during this period has been intensely cold, with biting East wind and snow. The YSER CANAL BEING Frozen.	
	JAN. 28th.		2nd Lieut A. D. PARKIN rejoined the Battalion from training reinforcements at the Base.	
	JAN. 29th.		One Man wounded by rifle bullet on a wiring party.	
	JAN. 30th.		The Battalion relieved the 17th Battalion Sherwood Foresters in the LEFT WIELTJE SECTION. The relief was carried out without incident. Battalion Headquarters were at HASLAR HOUSE ST. JEAN 2nd W. H. L. BULKELEY joined the Battalion. 2nd Lieut J. H. GOSLING returned from leave from ENGLAND.	

Lt. Colonel
Comdg. 16th Bn. Sherwood Foresters.

Army Form C. 2118.

WAR DIARY
or
INTELLIGENCE SUMMARY.
(Erase heading not required.)

16 Bn of Derby
Vol 12
12.A.

Place	Date	Hour	Summary of Events and Information	Remarks and references to Appendices
HASLAR HOUSE	Feb. 1st, 1917.		Lieut & Quartermaster A. F. LUNAM rejoined the Battalion from Sick Leave in England. Enemy Machine Guns were very active during the night. Enemy raided the 14th HAMPSHIRES on our right.	
	2nd.		2nd Lieut R. A. JOHNSON, M.C., invalided to ENGLAND.	
	3rd.		2nd Lieut J. HUTCHINSON joined the Battalion for duty.	
YPRES.	4th.		Major N. HOUGHTON assumed temporary command of the 17th BATTALION SHERWOOD FORESTERS, owing to Lieut Colonel H. M. MILWARD, D.S.O., being wounded. Enemy Aeroplanes crossed our lines on three occasions. The Battalion was relieved by the 1/1st HERTS REGIMENT. Three Companies proceeded into Support at YPRES, one Company at DRAGOON FARM, POTIJZE. Battalion Headquarters at THE CONVENT, YPRES. Lieut R. E. BURT joined the Battalion for duty.	
RAILWAY WOOD.	5th.		The Battalion relieved the 16th Rifle Brigade in the LEFT SUB-SECTION, RAILWAY WOOD. Enemy snipers were more active than usual. Our snipers claim two victims who were seen to fall.	
YPRES.	7th.		The Battalion was relieved by the 16th Rifle Brigade, and after relief proceeded to YPRES, with one Company at DRAGOON FARM, POTIJZE. Our Artillery has been actively engaged on wire cutting all day. Light Trench Mortars have registered on enemy wire this evening. Our Lewis Guns played on gaps cut in enemy wire all night of 6th. CASUALTIES :- One Man killed, two wounded.	
RAILWAY WOOD.	9th.		The Battalion relieved the 16th Rifle Brigade in the Left Sub-Section RAILWAY WOOD. CASUALTIES :- One Man wounded. From 9th to 12th February, our Artillery of all calibres has bombarded the enemies trenches from 9 a.m. to 4 p.m. daily. Drill Barrages lasting ten minutes have been put on each evening. Enemy has replied vigorously to our Shelling. CASUALTIES :- For the 9th, one Man wounded.	

Army Form C. 2118.

WAR DIARY
or
INTELLIGENCE SUMMARY.

(Erase heading not required.)

Instructions regarding War Diaries and Intelligence Summaries are contained in F.S. Regs., Part II. and the Staff Manual respectively. Title pages will be prepared in manuscript.

Place	Date	Hour	Summary of Events and Information	Remarks and references to Appendices
RAILWAY WOOD.	Feb. 10th.		Lieut. R. H. ELLIS transferred to ROYAL ENGINEERS, to date from December 6th, 1916. CASUALTIES :- 5 Other Ranks wounded. Heavy Artillery fire throughout the day.	
	11th.		The Commander-in-Chief awarded on behalf of the French Government, the following decorations :- "LA CROIX DE GUERRE." No. 26222, L/Sgt W. GYTE, for gallantry in the attack on SCHWABEN REDOUBT, October 9th, 1916. L/Sgt W. H. SHAW, attached to the 117th Machine Gun Coy. CASUALTIES :- 2 killed, and 8 Other Ranks wounded, including C.S.M. ONIONS. Draft of 75 Other Ranks arrived.	
	12th.		The 1st HERTS REGIMENT made a successful raid on our left, capturing 2 German Prisoners. During this raid, the enemy shelled our front line causing us casualties, 2 Killed, and 3 wounded.	
YPRES.	13th.		The Battalion was relieved on the evening of the 13th by the 16th RIFLE BRIGADE, and proceeded into Support billets in YPRES. A raid consisting of 4 Officers and 120 Other Ranks was carried out from our front by the 16th RIFLE BRIGADE on the enemy's front line trenches near THE MOUND. The 16th SHERWOOD FORESTERS were ordered to find the right flanking party. This consisted of 2nd Lieut W. A. MEDCALF and 31 Other Ranks, and 1 Lewis Gun and Team from "C" and "D" Companies. Sergeant JAYES and 15 men of "C" Company pushed up into an enemy Sap. No opposition was met with. The flanking party suffered 4 Casualties; all wounded by shell fire.	
"E" CAMP.	15th.		The Battalion was relieved by the 7th LIVERPOOL REGIMENT, and after relief marched to "E" Camp, near BRANDHOEK.	

Army Form C. 2118.

WAR DIARY
or
INTELLIGENCE SUMMARY.
(Erase heading not required.)

Instructions regarding War Diaries and Intelligence Summaries are contained in F.S. Regs., Part II. and the Staff Manual respectively. Title pages will be prepared in manuscript.

Place	Date	Hour	Summary of Events and Information	Remarks and references to Appendices
"E" CAMP	Feb. 15th		During the march, the enemy shelled the road. No Casualties.	
	16th		2nd Lieut. C. J. WELLS joined the Battalion for duty.	
			Draft of 48 Other Ranks arrived from the 39th Divisional Reinforcement Camp.	
	19th.		The Battalion commenced training at "E" Camp. Owing to the excellent facilities the Camp afforded, every man in the Battalion fired 10 rounds on the rifle range with Box Respirators on, and also fired a rifle grenade on the bombing ground. Inter-platoon and Inter-Company football matches were played daily.	
	21st.		2nd Lieut M. F. HASTINGS rejoined the Battalion from leave of absence in ENGLAND.	
	24th.		The 39th Division was transferred from the VIIIth to the Xth CORPS, Commanded by Lieut General Sir. T. MORLAND, K.C.B., K.B.M.G., D.S.O. The Battalion Football Team, having been reorganised, a game was arranged with the 17th KINGS ROYAL RIFLE CORPS. A fine victory was brought off by us, winning by 12 goals to Nil.	
	25th.		An Officers' Football Match was arranged against the 17th K.R.R.C. We lost by 2 goals to Nil. Draft of 81 Other Ranks arrived from the 39th Divisional Reinforcement Camp.	
	26th.		The Battalion entrained at BRANDHOEK STATION to relieve the 11th Bn NORTHUMBERLAND FUSILIERS in the Left ZILLEBEKE Sub-Section.	
ZILLE-BEKE.	27th.		Lieut R. W. LAWS rejoined the Battalion from Sick leave in ENGLAND.	

[signature] Lieut Colonel.
Commanding 16th Battalion Sherwood Foresters.

1/3/1917

16th (Service) Battalion Sherwood Foresters.

Army Form C. 2118.

WAR DIARY
or
INTELLIGENCE SUMMARY.
(Erase heading not required.)

Instructions regarding War Diaries and Intelligence Summaries are contained in F.S. Regs., Part II. and the Staff Manual respectively. Title pages will be prepared in manuscript.

Vol 13

13.A

Place	Date 1917.	Hour	Summary of Events and Information	Remarks and references to Appendices
ZILLEBEKE.	March 1st.		Lieut P. U. LAWS attached to 117th Infantry Brigade as Brigade Intelligence Officer.	
	3rd.		The Battalion was relieved in trenches by the 16th RIFLE BRIGADE and proceeded to the BARRACKS, YPRES, becoming Battalion in Divisional Reserve. During this tour in trenches from February 26th to March 3rd, the enemy was very quiet: we suffered no casualties.	
BARRACKS. YPRES.	4th.		BRIGADIER-GENERAL R. D. F. OLDMAN, D.S.O., relinquished command of the 117th Infantry Brigade, and proceeded to ENGLAND to command a Reserve Infantry Brigade. Lieut Colonel C. HERBERT STEPNEY, D.S.O., assumed temporary command of the Brigade. Captain S. F. LILLEY took over command of the Battalion.	
	6th.		The First Anniversary dinner celebrating the arrival of the Battalion in FRANCE was held at the BARRACKS, YPRES. The following Officers who came out with the Battalion were present. Lieut Colonel C. HERBERT STEPNEY, D.S.O. Major M. HOUGHTON. Captain S. F. LILLEY. " R. F. TRUSCOTT. " R. L. ILLINGWORTH, M.C. " D. H. COHEN. " P. H. COLERIDGE, M.C. " H. R. STEVENS, M.C. Lieut P. U. LAWS. " D. W. STEVENS, M.C. 2nd Lieut A. D. PARKIN. Rev. A. P. DANIELS, M.C.	
	7.		Captain R. F. TRUSCOTT attached to 117th Infantry Brigade. Captain S. J. L. LINDEMAN, R.A.M.C., rejoined the Battalion from Sick leave in ENGLAND. 2nd Lieut C. F. BOWER promoted LIEUTENANT with effect from December 7th, 1916.	

Army Form C. 2118.

16th (Service) Battalion Sherwood Foresters.

WAR DIARY
or
INTELLIGENCE SUMMARY.
(Erase heading not required.)

Instructions regarding War Diaries and Intelligence Summaries are contained in F. S. Regs., Part II. and the Staff Manual respectively. Title pages will be prepared in manuscript.

Place	Date 1917.	Hour	Summary of Events and Information	Remarks and references to Appendices
BARRACKS. YPRES.	March. 8th.		2nd Lieut L. M. HARRISON joined the Battalion on first appointment. Major N. HOUGHTON rejoined Battalion on relinquishing command of the 17th Battalion Sherwood Foresters.	
	9th.		BRIGADIER-GENERAL G. A. ARMYTAGE. D.S.O., assumed command of the 117th Infantry Brigade. Lieut Colonel C. HERBERT STEPNEY. D.S.O., assumed command of the Battalion.	
	10th.		At 4 a.m., the Battalion was relieved by the 4/5th BLACK WATCH in the BARRACKS, YPRES, and on being relieved marched to TORONTO CAMP near OUDERDOM, into CORPS RESERVE. Captain D. H. COHEN appointed Staff Captain, 117th Infantry Brigade.	
TORONTO CAMP.	11th.		Lieut-General Sir. T. L. MORLAND, K.C.B.,K.C.M.G.,D.S.O., visited the Battalion at TORONTO CAMP. Major N. Houghton proceeded on leave in FRANCE.	
	13th.		The Battalion played 17th Battalion Sherwood Foresters at football, winning by 6 goals to nil. A concert was held in the Y.M.C.A., Hut at TORONTO CAMP.	
	14th.		GENERAL SIR H. C. O. PLUMER, G.C.M.G.,K.C.B.,A.D.C., Commanding 2nd ARMY, inspected the Battalion and expressed his satisfaction on the turn out and soldierly appearance of all ranks on parade.	
ZILLEBEKE.	15th.		The Battalion moved from BRANDHOEK by train to YPRES relieving the 1/1st HERTS REGIMENT in the LEFT SUB-SECTION (HOOGE) The enemy was very quiet during this tour in trenches from 15th March to 21st March, our casualties amounting to two Other Ranks wounded.	

1577 Wt.W10791/1773 500,000 1/15 D.D.&L.   A.D.S.S./Forms/C. 2118.

Army Form C. 2118.

16th (Service) Battalion Sherwood Foresters.

WAR DIARY
or
INTELLIGENCE SUMMARY.

(Erase heading not required.)

Instructions regarding War Diaries and Intelligence Summaries are contained in F. S. Regs., Part II. and the Staff Manual respectively. Title pages will be prepared in manuscript.

Place	Date 1917.	Hour	Summary of Events and Information	Remarks and references to Appendices
ZILLEBEKE.	March 15th.		About 650 coils of wire were put out by the Battalion forming a new belt.	
	19th.		2nd Lieut A. D. PARKIN and Rev. A. P. DANIELS M.C. proceeded on leave to the UNITED KINGDOM.	
BARRACKS YPRES.	21st.		The Battalion was relieved by the 16th RIFLE BRIGADE in the LEFT SUB-SECTION and became the Battalion in Divisional Reserve at the BARRACKS, YPRES. 2nd Lieut E. N. SMITH joined the Battalion. A draft of 67 Other Ranks arrived.	
	22nd.		2nd Lieut A. L. HOLLAND. M.C., invalided to ENGLAND. Captain L. H. ASKWITH granted leave to ENGLAND.	
	23rd.		Lieut P. U. LAWS promoted Captain with effect from March 11th, 1917. 2nd Lieut T. C. G. WILLIAMS promoted LIEUTENANT with effect from March 12th, 1917.	
	24th.		Major N. HOUGHTON returned from leave from PARIS.	
	25th.		A draft of 17 Other Ranks arrived.	
	26th.		Act. Lieut S. W. HILL, and 2nd Lieut E. S. ESAM, transferred to 117th Light Trench Mortar Battery.	
WINNIPEG CAMP.	27th.		The Battalion was relieved by the 4/5th BLACK WATCH and after relief marched to WINNIPEG CAMP.	

1577 Wt.W10791/1773 300,000 1/15 D. D. & L. A.D.S.S./Forms/C. 2118.

16th (Service) Battalion Sherwood Foresters.

Army Form C. 2118.

WAR DIARY
or
INTELLIGENCE SUMMARY.
(*Erase heading not required.*)

Instructions regarding War Diaries and Intelligence Summaries are contained in F. S. Regs., Part II. and the Staff Manual respectively. Title pages will be prepared in manuscript.

Place	Date 1917.	Hour	Summary of Events and Information	Remarks and references to Appendices
WINNIPEG CAMP.	March 28th.		Lieut R. URE, and 2nd Lieut. R. E. BURT, invalided to ENGLAND.	
	31st.		2nd Lieut A. D. PARKIN and Rev. A. P. DANIELS M.C. returned from leave in ENGLAND.	

Lieut Colonel.

Commanding 16th (Ser) Battalion Sherwood Foresters.

March 31st, 1917.

16th (Service) Battalion Sherwood Foresters.

WAR DIARY
or
INTELLIGENCE SUMMARY.

(Erase heading not required.)

Army Form C. 2118.

Instructions regarding War Diaries and Intelligence Summaries are contained in F.S. Regs., Part II. and the Staff Manual respectively. Title pages will be prepared in manuscript.

Place	Date 1917.	Hour	Summary of Events and Information	Remarks and references to Appendices
WINNIPEG CAMP.	APRIL 1st.		Lieut Colonel C. HERBERT STEPNEY, D.S.O., proceeded on leave to ENGLAND.	
	2nd.		Major N. HOUGHTON assumed command of the Battalion.	
	3rd.		The Battalion Football Eleven played the 235th HOWITZER BATTERY Eleven, losing 2 goals to 1.	
BARRACKS YPRES.	3rd.		The Battalion relieved the 1st CAMBRIDGESHIRE REGIMENT in THE BARRACKS, YPRES.	
	4th.		Captain L. H. ASKWITH returned from leave in ENGLAND.	
SANCTUARY WOOD.	6th.		The Battalion relieved the 11th ROYAL SUSSEX REGIMENT in the TORR TOP - SANCTUARY WOOD SECTOR.	
	7th.		Captain R. L. ILLINGWORTH, M.C. proceeded to the 2nd Army School of Instruction at LISQUES.	
	9th.		This tour in the trenches was quiet until the 9th, when the Enemy heavily bombarded the Sector on our right for the whole day, and at 6.30 p.m. made a daylight raid on the front occupied by the 11th Battalion SHERWOOD FORESTERS. Our front was not affected except in the neighbourhood of MAPLE COPSE, where the approaches to the front line were shelled.	
			Casualties :- Two wounded.	
	10th.		Two killed, Five wounded.	
	11th.		Captain S. F. LILLEY proceeded on leave to ENGLAND. The Battalion was relieved by the 14th HAMPSHIRE REGIMENT and proceeded by train from the ASYLUM STATION, YPRES, to BRANDHOEK - "B" Camp, arriving at 6.0 a.m. (12th inst.)	
BRANDHOEK - MERCKEGHEM	14th.		The Battalion proceeded by train from POPERINGHE to ESQUELBECQUE, thence by route march to billets at MERCKEGHEM.	

Army Form C. 2118.

16th (Service) Battalion Sherwood Foresters.

WAR DIARY
or
INTELLIGENCE SUMMARY.

(Erase heading not required.)

Instructions regarding War Diaries and Intelligence Summaries are contained in F. S. Regs., Part II. and the Staff Manual respectively. Title pages will be prepared in manuscript.

Place	Date	Hour	Summary of Events and Information	Remarks and references to Appendices
MARCK GHEM.	APRIL 1917. 15th.		Major H. A. LEGGETT rejoined the Battalion from the 39th Divisional Reinforcement Camp.	
	16th.		Battalion training commenced. Draft of 5 Other Ranks. The Division returned to the "11th CORPS"	
	17th.		Draft of 29 Other Ranks. 28 men sent to work on farms in the vicinity.	
	18th.		Rev. A. P. DANIELS proceeded to ENGLAND on being transferred to do duty with the MESOPOTAMIAN FORCES.	
	19th.		Lieut Colonel C. HERBERT STEPNEY. D.S.O., returned from leave in ENGLAND.	
	21st.		The Battalion was inspected in the ATTACK by Major-General G. J. CUTHBERT, C.B.,C.M.G., Commanding 39th Division. Brigade Concert. 2nd Lieut G. R. MACDONALD reported for duty.	
	22nd.		Brigade Church Parade. the 39th Divisional Band in attendance. 39th Divisional Band played from 5.0 p.m. to 6.30 p.m.	
	23rd.		The Battalion was inspected by the SURGEON GENERAL of the 2nd ARMY.	
	25th.		The Battalion was inspected in THE ATTACK by GENERAL SIR HERBERT C. O. PLUMER, G.C.M.G., K.C.B.,A.D.C., Commanding 2nd Army. 2nd Lieut F. G. GRAVES reported for duty.	

A6945 Wt.W1422/M160 35,000 12/16 D.D.&L. Forms/C./2118/14.

Army Form C. 2118.

16th (Service) Battalion Sherwood Foresters.

WAR DIARY
or
INTELLIGENCE SUMMARY.
(Erase heading not required.)

Instructions regarding War Diaries and Intelligence Summaries are contained in F. S. Regs., Part II. and the Staff Manual respectively. Title pages will be prepared in manuscript.

Place	Date	Hour	Summary of Events and Information	Remarks and references to Appendices
MERCKEGHEM.	April 26th.		No. 6 Platoon, commanded by 2nd Lieutenant W. E. WRIGHT, came out first in the Brigade Inter-Platoon Competition. The result of the Brigade Signalling Test showed that we have :-	
			3 Qualified Instructors.	
			9 First Class Signallers.	
			3 Second Class Signallers.	
"L" CAMP.	27th.		The Battalion marched to ESQUELBECQUE and proceeded by train to POPERINGHE, and thence by march route to "L" Camp on the CROMM ROAD, 3 miles north of POPERINGHE. "B" Company moved to PROVEN to work on Water Supply works. Captain S. F. LILLEY returned from leave in ENGLAND.	
BRANDHOEK.	28th.		The three Companies moved from "L" Camp to tents near BRANDHOEK, and commenced work on Railways in the vicinity. "B" Company remained at PROVEN.	
	29th.		The Battalion worked from 2.0 a.m. to 5.0 a.m., and from 5.0 p.m. to 9.0 p.m. on Railway work	
	30th.		Lieut D. E. BULL transferred to a LABOUR BATTALION at BOULOGNE. Lieut T. L. DARBYSHIRE took over the duties of TRANSPORT OFFICER. Brigadier-General G. A. ARMYTAGE, D.S.O., Commanding 117th Infantry Brigade, presented at PROVEN, the banner won by No. 6 Platoon for being the best platoon in the Brigade.	

May 1st, 1917.

Lieut Colonel.
Commanding 16th Battalion Sherwood Foresters.

Army Form C. 2118.

16th (Service) Battalion Sherwood Foresters.
WAR DIARY
or
INTELLIGENCE SUMMARY.
(Erase heading not required.)

Instructions regarding War Diaries and Intelligence Summaries are contained in F. S. Regs., Part II. and the Staff Manual respectively. Title pages will be prepared in manuscript.

Place	Date	Hour	Summary of Events and Information	Remarks and references to Appendices
BRANDHOEK. "O" Camp.	1917. May. 1st.		The Battalion moved into "O" Camp near BRANDHOEK. "B" Company rejoined the Battalion from PROVEN. 500 men per day employed on Railway Construction. Division moved into the adjoining Camp, "D" Camp.	
	2nd.		No. 6 Platoon was sent to the Brigade Platoon School. No. 2 Platoon played No. 6 Platoon at football. No. 2 won. Result :- 1 goal - nil. Captain P. H. COLERIDGE, M.C., took command of the Brigade Platoon School with 2nd Lieut W. E. WRIGHT as assistant instructor.	
	3rd.		Brigade Concert attended by the Divisional and Brigade Generals.	
	4th.		No. 11 Platoon and No. 16 Platoon at football. No. 16 Platoon won; result 3 goals - 2. 2nd Anniversary of the Battalion's formation.	
	5th.		No. 2 Platoon versus No. 16 Platoon at football. No. 2 Platoon won; result 1 goal - nil. 2nd Lieutenants G. R. MACDONALD, J. HUTCHINSON, and E. N. SMITH, transferred to the 2/8th Battalion SHERWOOD FORESTERS.	
	6th.		Brigadier General G. A. ARMYTAGE, D.S.O., dined with the Battalion Headquarter Officers. No. 2 Platoon versus 117th Machine Gun Company at football. Draw: two goals each side. Played extra time with no further result.	
	7th.		2nd Lieut G. F. GIBSON reported for duty and posted to "B" Company.	
	8th.		No. 2 Platoon played the 117th Machine Gun Company at football. Result - No 2 Platoon won. 2 goals - 1.	
	9th.		Captain C. H. L. RIXON, R.A.M.C., relieved Captain S. J. L. LINDEMAN, R.A.M.C., as Medical Officer of the Battalion, the latter being transferred to the 133rd Field Ambulance.	15A

Army Form C. 2118.

WAR DIARY
or
INTELLIGENCE SUMMARY.
(Erase heading not required.)

Instructions regarding War Diaries and Intelligence Summaries are contained in F. S. Regs., Part II. and the Staff Manual respectively. Title pages will be prepared in manuscript.

Place	Date	Hour	Summary of Events and Information	Remarks and references to Appendices
	1917. May. 10th.			
	11th.		The Transport was inspected by Lieut Colonel PARSONS, Officer Commanding 39th Divisional Train.	
			Battalion Sports were held to decide the competitors who would represent the Battalion in the Brigade Sports, to be held the following day.	
	12th.		The Brigade Concert Party gave their first concert.	
	13th.		Brigade Sports were held near "C" Camp. (BRANDHOEK VIC INTY) The "100 yards" and "Mile" races were won by Pte LOWE "C" Coy. Staff Sergeant POLLARD. respectively.	
			2nd Lieut A. ROBINSON reported for duty and posted to "C" Company.	
			2nd Lieut A. S. Mellor proceeded on leave to England.	
			The A.D.M.S. dined with Headquarter Officers.	
	14th.		Lieut F. P. HOLMES took over charge of the TRANSPORT in the absence of Lieut T. L. DARBYSHIRE sent to Field Ambulance with Trench Fever.	
			Sergeant F. SARGEANT promoted Company Sergeant Major of "A" Company.	
HILL TOP SECTOR.	15th.		The Battalion marched at 9.30.p.m. from "O" Camp to the USER CANAL BANK, becoming Battalion in Left Reserve to the HILL TOP SECTOR.	
CANAL BANK.	16th.		16 men left isolated at "O" Camp owing to one man having measles.	
			The Battalion supplied Three Hundred men for work in the HILL TOP SECTOR.	
			A "C" Company dugout was blown in by direct hit - no casualties	

Army Form C. 2118.

WAR DIARY
or
INTELLIGENCE SUMMARY.
(Erase heading not required.)

Instructions regarding War Diaries and Intelligence
Summaries are contained in F. S. Regs., Part II.
and the Staff Manual respectively. Title pages
will be prepared in manuscript.

Place	Date	Hour	Summary of Events and Information	Remarks and references to Appendices
	MAY. 18th.		The Battalion was detailed for work in constructing a new trench to be called BELLINGHAM TRENCH, in advance of FORWARD COTTAGE GAP, to the NORTH of HILL TOP FARM.	
			The work, under the command of Lieut. Colonel C. HERBERT STEPNEY, D.S.O.; was carried out by the 225th FIELD COY. R.E., the 13th GLOSTER PIONEER BATTALION, and the 16th BATTALION SHERWOOD FORESTERS.	
			At 9.30 p.m., the enemy commenced a very heavy barrage on this sector, causing a few casualties, and wounding Lieut HOLLEY, R.E., and his sergeant, who were to have taped out the line of the new trench. No casualties were inflicted on this battalion, however, and work on the trench was commenced at 11.0 p.m., and continued until 4.0 a.m., when the excavation of the trench was nearly complete.	
	19th.		Captain P. H. COLERIDGE, M.C., proceeded on leave to ENGLAND.	
			Three platoons continued to work on the new BELLINGHAM trench.	
	21st.		2nd Lieut G. SABINE reported for duty and was attached to "D" Company.	
			2nd Lieut W.H.L. BULKELEY, proceeded on leave to ENGLAND.	
			Company Sergeant Major COKAYNE reported for duty and posted to "C" Coy.	
	22nd.		The Lewis Gun Teams of the Battalion relieved those of the 17th Battalion SHERWOOD FORESTERS in the front line of the HILL TOP SECTOR.	
HILL TOP SECTOR.	23rd.		The Battalion relieved the 17th Battalion SHERWOOD FORESTERS in the front line HILL TOP SECTOR. Battalion Headquarters at LA BELLE ALLIANCE, "B" Company on the Left, "C" Company on the Right. "A" Company Left Support, and "D" Company RIGHT SUPPORT.	
	25th.		One of our Snipers claimed a victim.	
			Major N. HOUGHTON, Regimental Sergeant Major J. PEPPER, Company Sergeant Major TURNEY; Private CROSSLAND (Attached to 117th Trench Mortar Battery) were Mentioned in Despatches.	

Army Form C. 2118.

WAR DIARY
or
INTELLIGENCE SUMMARY.
(Erase heading not required.)

Instructions regarding War Diaries and Intelligence Summaries are contained in F.S. Regs., Part II. and the Staff Manual respectively. Title pages will be prepared in manuscript.

Place	Date	Hour	Summary of Events and Information	Remarks and references to Appendices
	MAY. 26th.		Lieut Colonel C. HERBERT STEPNEY, D.S.O., Mentioned in Despatches.	
			Lieutenant P. E. Burrows, M.C., promoted Captain. 2nd Lieutenants A. D. PARKIN, F. H. GOSLING, W. J. HASTINGS, C. E. GARLAND, promoted Lieutenants.	
			Lieutenant F. P. Holmes, proceeded on leave to ENGLAND.	
			The Left Front Company ("B" Company) was heavily shelled with heavy MINENWERFER on their left, island posts. A gap of about 20 feet was made in one of the posts.	
	27th.		From 12 noon to 4 p.m. the enemy shelled the island N.W. of TURCO FARM with MINENWERFER doing a considerable amount of damage and completely obliterating one of the posts. Casualties:- 1 man killed, 2 wounded. One Lewis Gun was put out of action.	
			2nd Lieut B. T. McPHERSON took over the duties of Transport Officer.	
	28th.		At 3.30 a.m., having breached our parapet and wire by the MINENWERFER bombardment of the two preceeding days, the enemy effected a raid on our front line to the NORTH of TURCO FARM. The raiding party was 50 strong and attacked No. 11 Post probably taking two prisoners. One of these, Private CHARLESWORTH succeeded in making his escape and returned. The other is still missing. Although attacked, the Lewis Gun teams succeeded in keeping up fire, and at least two of the enemy were left in No Man's Land. Another who lost his way was subsequently captured by us.	
			Our Casualties during this raid - 1 wounded, 1 missing.	
			Casualties later in the day, 1 killed, and 1 wounded.	
	29th.		At 11.15 a.m., the enemy shelled TURCO FARM with forty 4.2 shells.	
			2nd Lieut G. F. GIBSON admitted to Field Ambulance.	

Army Form C. 2118.

WAR DIARY
or
INTELLIGENCE SUMMARY.
(Erase heading not required.)

Instructions regarding War Diaries and Intelligence Summaries are contained in F. S. Regs., Part II. and the Staff Manual respectively. Title pages will be prepared in manuscript.

Place	Date	Hour	Summary of Events and Information	Remarks and references to Appendices
	MAY.			
	30th.		TURCO FARM again shelled.	
			38th Divisional Machine Gun Company fired 15 Machine Guns from 6.0 p.m. to 6.15 p.m. on to enemy back areas. The enemy replied by shelling TURCO FARM and HILL TOP FARM, with about fifty shells -- mainly 10 cm, and 7.7 cm.	
	31st.		Major H. A. LEGGETT, and Captain A. STEVENSON, M.C., were wounded (slightly) and admitted to Field Ambulance.	
BRANDHOEK. "O" Camp.	1.6.1917.		The Battalion was relieved by the 11th Battalion ROYAL SUSSEX REGIMENT, and proceeded by march route to "O" Camp near BRANDHOEK.	

Archd. McQuay   Lieut Colonel.
Commanding 16th. Battalion Sherwood Foresters.

Headquarters.
    117th Infantry Brigade.

    I have to report that the enemy raided my line N.W. of TURCO FARM at 3-30am this morning.

    He came over between Nos.11(a) and 12 Posts about 50 strong. No.11(a) Post which is held only by night had just been withdrawn.

    He attacked No.11 Post, which was held by 1 N.C.O and 6 men

    He seems to have taken two men of this post prisoners and then retired across NO MAN'S LAND to CALEDONIA TRENCH. One of the prisoners (Pte CHARLESWORTH) however effected his escape in NO MAN'S LAND and has rejoined.

    Our Lewis Gun at No.10 Post fired 36 drums at the raiders as they retired across NO MAN'S LAND and they claim to have accounted for a number of the enemy who were seen to fall.

    No.11 Post has been much damaged by shell fire and the parapet breached, and is at present untenable.

    The affair was over in a few minutes. The Germans did not remain more than 3 or 4 minutes in our line.

    Our casualties were 2 men wounded, 1 missing.

May 28th 1917.   sd. C.Herbert Stepney, Lt.Col.
8 a.m.   Commanding 16th Sherwood Foresters.

16it 13th SHERWOOD FORESTERS.
WAR DIARY for the Month of JUNE. 39 1/7

WAR DIARY
INTELLIGENCE SUMMARY
(Erase heading not required.)

Place	Date	Hour	Summary of Events and Information	Remarks and references to Appendices
'O' CAMP. near BRANDHOEK	JUNE 1/6/17		The Battalion found working parties for the 7th CANADIAN TUNNELLING COY.	
"	2nd		CAPT. R. L. ILLINGWORTH. M.C. proceeded on leave to ENGLAND	
"	4th		The Battalion football team played 11th 13th SHERWOOD FORESTERS at TORONTO CAMP. resulting in a win for the Battalion – 3 goals – 1 goal. The Brigade Concert Party gave their second concert at C. CAMP.	
"	6th		Capt & Adjutant S. F. LILLEY awarded the MILITARY CROSS – KING'S BIRTHDAY HONOUR LIST – London Gazette JUNE. 4. 1917. New Draft. H. Other Ranks	
"	7th		The Battalion football team played the 17th Bn NORTHUMBERLAND FUSILIERS at C. CAMP. resulting in a win for the Battalion. 4 goals – 1. The Lewis Gun teams of B and C. Coys relieved the teams of the 17th Bn SHERWOOD FORESTERS in the WIELTJE SECTOR (ST. JEAN.) (One man wounded)	

16A

WAR DIARY or INTELLIGENCE SUMMARY.

Army Form C. 2118.

Place	Date	Hour	Summary of Events and Information	Remarks and references to Appendices
WIELTJE. ST. JEAN.	JUNE 8th		The Battalion less D. Coy and three platoons of A. Coy. relieved 2½ Coys of the 17 Bn. SHERWOOD FORESTERS in the front line WIELTJE SECTOR, becoming attached to the 116th Infantry Brigade, C. Coy. on the right, B. Coy. on the left and two platoons of A. Coy. under Lieut. PARKIN in reserve. Battalion Headquarters was at HASLER HOUSE, ST. JEAN. The remaining 6 platoons under the command of CAPT. C. G. LORD remained at C. CAMP near BRANDHOEK supplying working parties for the 7. CANADIAN TUNNELLING COY. At 11.19.p.m. the relief having been completed by 10.30.p.m. we discharged gas projected and bombarded the enemy's lines. He retaliated heavily with MINENWERFER and 5.9" shells. ARMYTAGE TRENCH suffered most severely, being bombarded from 11.15 pm until dawn, causing casualties as under:- Killed:- 3/1773. L/Cpl. COMERY. E., 76479. Pte LEWIS. W. H., 76148. Pte DUFTON. J., 41853. Pte HOWE. E. J., Wounded:- 12712. Pte GARROD. E., 76123. Pte COOPER. M., 52933. Pte BENSON. E., 42204. Pte BOOTH. J., 58430. Pte PIMM. H. J.,	

WAR DIARY
or
INTELLIGENCE SUMMARY.
(Erase heading not required.)

Army Form C. 2118.

Place	Date	Hour	Summary of Events and Information	Remarks and references to Appendices
MELTJE.	JUNE 9th		The enemy shelled ST JEAN with 10.cm shells wounding the sentry on duty — 32558. Pte. HYDE. W., and obtaining a direct hit on a dugout killing one man and wounding two — lists above.	
			The V Army commanded by GEN SIR H du L P GOUGH K.C.B took over the front held by the VIII CORPS 2nd ARMY	
	10th		ARMITAGE. TR was again heavily shelled until 2.0am causing further casualties:— Killed — 11787 A/Cpl. MASKERY. H.P., 70561. Pte. HIGGINGBOTTOM. C., Wounded — 27301 A/Cpl. DOWSING. R.L., 76157. Pte. EGAN. A., 71545. Pte. SALMON. E., This bombardment was repeated from 11.0 pm until dawn on the 11th when	
	11th		further casualties were caused by a very heavy MINENWERFER bombardment lasting one hour & three quarters. Wounded — 56485. Pte. FOX. R., 27831. Pte. SHAW. T., 16153. Pte. FARMER. H., 26181. Pte. OWENS. B.H., 17027 Pte. BLOOMER. A. wounded.	
	12.		A quiet day.	
	13.		From midnight (night of 12/13th.) until 5.0 am the enemy sent over a large number of gas shells between ST JEAN and YPRES. A certain number fell in ST JEAN	

Army Form C. 2118.

WAR DIARY
or
INTELLIGENCE SUMMARY.
(Erase heading not required.)

Instructions regarding War Diaries and Intelligence Summaries are contained in F. S. Regs., Part II. and the Staff Manual respectively. Title pages will be prepared in manuscript.

Place	Date	Hour	Summary of Events and Information	Remarks and references to Appendices
	JUNE.			
HIELTJE	13th contin.		The 39th Division came under the command of the XVIII Corps commanded by Gen. SIR F. IVOR MAXSE, K.C.B., C.V.O., D.S.O.	
			During the evening the enemy sent over two 8" and several 5.9" shells into ST. JEAN. causing an R.E. Dump to catch on fire. A great many trench boards, sandbags, STOKES MORTAR BOMBS and S.A.A. were destroyed. Much assistance was rendered by R.S.M. PEPPER who did much to stop the spread of the fire and displayed great initiative and gallantry under heavy shell fire.	
			Casualties:- Wounded - 25545. R.S.M. PEPPER.T. 55169. Pte. DEGG.T. 26064. Pte. ARMSTRONG.A. 27506. Pte. ROOME.W.	☒
	14th		Quiet day & night. 71129 Pte. BIRCH. A. wounded	☒
	15th		The Battalion was relieved by the 9th Bn. KING'S (LIVERPOOL REGT.) and proceeded to the CANAL BANK becoming the Battalion in fyfe Support to the HILL TOP SECTOR.	
			During this tour in the HIELTJE SECTOR the total casualties were 6 Killed. 20 wounded. A New Draft arrived = 1 Corporal. 3 Lance Corporals. 13 Privates	☒

Army Form C. 2118.

WAR DIARY
or
INTELLIGENCE SUMMARY.
(Erase heading not required.)

Instructions regarding War Diaries and Intelligence Summaries are contained in F. S. Regs., Part II. and the Staff Manual respectively. Title pages will be prepared in manuscript.

Place	Date	Hour	Summary of Events and Information	Remarks and references to Appendices
YSER. CANAL BANK	JUNE 16th		CAPT. P.E. BURROWS. M.C. proceeded on leave to ENGLAND.	
			The Battalion commenced supplying working parties for the 13 Bn. GLOSTER REGT. and 225. FIELD COY. R.E.	
			The 117 Infantry Brigade moved into the HILL TOP SECTOR relieving the 116 Infantry Brigade.	
	18th.		Lt. Col. C. HERBERT. STEPNEY. D.S.O. took over the command of the 117th Infantry Brigade during the temporary absence of BRIG. GEN. G.A. ARMYTAGE. D.S.O. on leave in ENGLAND. MAJOR N. HOUGHTON assumed command of the Battalion.	
			2nd Lieut. F.N. BEWLEY reported for duty & was posted to 'B'. COY.	
	19th		2nd Lieutenants J.G. MORRIS and C.E. ROBINSON reported for duty & were posted to B & C Coys respectively.	
	21st		The CANAL BANK was shelled with 5.9" & 4.2" shells.	
			Casualties — Two Killed. 55281. PTE. CLARKE J.E. 163349. PTE. ATKINSON. F.O.	

Army Form C. 2118.

WAR DIARY
or
INTELLIGENCE SUMMARY.
(Erase heading not required.)

Instructions regarding War Diaries and Intelligence Summaries are contained in F. S. Regs., Part II. and the Staff Manual respectively. Title pages will be prepared in manuscript.

Place	Date	Hour	Summary of Events and Information	Remarks and references to Appendices
HILL TOP	June 24th		The Battalion relieved the 17.B: SHERWOOD FORESTERS in the front line, HILL TOP SECTOR taking over a "One company" front. D.Coy. - front line., A.Coy - LA BELLE ALLIANCE., C.Coy. - at Battalion Headquarters., B.Coy. - 2 Platoons at IRISH FARM and 2 Platoons on the CANAL BANK. During the night the enemy shelled the whole front. Casualties. Eleven wounded :- 26408. L/Cpl. MOULDS. G., 76354. Pte. BROWN. A., 76352. Pte. BANTLE. J., 60078. Pte. KILBOURNE. G., 53544. Pte. WILKINSON. H., 54638. Pte. LAWSON. A., [illegible], 31740. Pte. DAINTY. E., 71554. Pte. WHITEHEAD. G., 32366. Pte. GREENHALL. K., 51610. Pte. SYKES. W., 71498. Pte. DAVIES. C.,	
	25th		The enemy shelled A.Coy. and Battalion Headquarters with 5.9" and 4.2" shells both afternoon and evening. Casualties:- 14 wounded :- 26020. Pte. SAXTON. O., 54386. Pte. FLETCHER. G.H., 7845. Pte. CLAYTON. W., 52907. Pte. NOSELEY. E., 45646. Pte. DRURY. G., 42095. Pte. HAWLEY. J., 70124. Pte. GREEN. E.B., 46647. Pte. PICK. H., 25920. Pte. CANWELL. G.F., 25816. Pte. WILSON. J.T.W., 26889. L/Cpl. MARSH. H.W. 76126. L/Cpl. COUGLE. W., 23112. Pte. SHATWELL. W., 71537. Pte. RAISON. W.A. [illegible] R.S.M. PEPPER was awarded the MILITARY CROSS for GALLANTRY IN THE FIELD.	

WAR DIARY
or
INTELLIGENCE SUMMARY.
(Erase heading not required.)

Army Form C. 2118.

Place	Date	Hour	Summary of Events and Information	Remarks and references to Appendices
HILL TOP	June 26		HILL TOP, BILGE TR., and CONEY ST. were shelled with 5.9" & 4.2" shells. During the evening Battalion Headquarters was shelled with similar calibres. Casualties 5 wounded: - 26668 Sgt. OLERENSHAW. N., ~~11175 Pte BILEY. G.~~, 27493 Pte PARKER. S.R., 67097 C.S.M. SARGENT. F., 129044 L/Cpl BRITLAND. A., 26844 Pte THOMPSON. A.,	
	27		HILL TOP was again shelled with 5.9" & 4.2" shells and at midnight the enemy opened out a heavy MINENWERFER and TRENCH MORTAR barrage. Retaliation was given by 4.5" and 6" howitzers. Casualties 1 killed 3 wounded:- 14241 Pte RICHARDSON. R. - killed. Wounded: - 71947 Pte OWEN. G., 26105 Pte HUDSON. G.I., 7154 Pte SWIRE. F., 2nd Lieut G.F. WHITE reported for duty & was posted to D Coy.	
	28th		Intermittent shelling of Battalion Headquarters during the whole day. Several MINENWERFER on BILGE TR. at midnight. Casualties 16 wounded:- CAPT. C.G. LORD, LIEUT. W.J. HASTINGS (both wounded at duty), 32475 Pte CAWKILL. J., 25742 Sgt. UNDERWOOD. C., 6590. Pte CLAYTON. H., 76115. Pte BEATTIE. J., 71948. Pte SEARSON. A., 20468. L/Cpl. MOSLEY. W.H., 32450 Pte MOORBY. W.E., 47833 L/Cpl. SPENCER. J.S., 24296. Pte RUSSELL. E., 71126. Pte WEBBERLEY. E.A., 71524. Pte HOLMES. J., 7112. Pte FALLOWS. J., 15748. Sgt POLLARD. L., 27091 Pte VINATT. S., 25281. Pte RICHARDS. A., ~~11757 Cpl SHELTON~~ 25904 Cpl WILSON. E.H.,	

WAR DIARY
or
INTELLIGENCE SUMMARY.
(Erase heading not required.)

Army Form C. 2118.

Place	Date	Hour	Summary of Events and Information	Remarks and references to Appendices
HILL TOP	June 29th		The enemy heavily shelled HILL TOP with 5.9" shells. Battalion Headquarters also received attention with shells of similar calibre. The Lewis Guns Teams were relieved by the teams of the 1/1 CAMBRIDGESHIRE REGT. Casualties :- Wounded :- 7605. Pte. MALKINSON. C., 26805. Pte. HURNER. A., 31847. Pte. DENNIS. F.W., 17684. Pte. MELLOR. I.N., 47836. Pte. MARTIN. P., 26710. Cpl. CLEMENTS. S.W., 74452 Pte BRIERLEY. S.H.	
	30th		The Battalion was relieved by the 1/1st CAMBRIDGESHIRE REGT. and proceeded to 'O' CAMP near BRANDHOEK. Casualties :- Killed :- 10441 Pte. HAGGER. H, 40006. Pte. TRAYNOR. R.T. 2 Wounded 25887 Pte. WALTHAM. J.W., 24159. Pte. TAYNOR. W.	

Major
Commanding
16 SHERWOOD FORESTERS

16th Battalion SHERWOOD FORESTERS

WAR DIARY
or
INTELLIGENCE SUMMARY.
(Erase heading not required.)

Army Form C. 2118.

Place	Date	Hour	Summary of Events and Information	Remarks and references to Appendices
SERQUES	July 1st		The Battalion marched from O Camp to POPERINGHE and proceeded by train to WATTEN, thence by route march to billets at MOULLE and SERQUES - two miles N.W. of ST OMER.	
"	2nd		Lieut. Col. C. HERBERT STEPNEY D.S.O. resumed Command of the Battalion on the return of BRIG. GEN. G.A. ARMITAGE A.S.O. from leave in ENGLAND.	
"	3rd		The day was devoted to rest and cleaning up	
"	4th		During the morning the Battalion was employed in digging Trenches the rest in Training	
"	5th		Coys were inspected by the Commanding Officer and Brigade and Company Training Carried out. Major H.A. LEGGETT proceeded to ETAPLES as the Finder of Reinforcements at No 3 Training Camp.	
"			Lieut. T.J. DARBYSHIRE struck off the strength of the Battalion during the period training at Rollencourt	
"			on the Vickers Gun for the Brigade	
"	8th		The Battalion Football Team played the 9th Battalion SHERWOOD FORESTERS and won their Group by 5 Goals - nil	
"			Ames resulted in a win for us 5 Goals - Nil	
"			The Rev. T.F. BLOXHAM was attached to the Battalion as successor to the Rev. A.P. DANIELS.	
"	13th		The Battalion took part in a Brigade BRIGADE DAWN ATTACK on the Training Ground	

16th Battalion SHERWOOD FORESTERS.

WAR DIARY
or
INTELLIGENCE SUMMARY.

Army Form C. 2118.

Place	Date	Hour	Summary of Events and Information	Remarks and references to Appendices
SERQUES	1917 July 4th		The Battalion took part in a Brigade Divisional attack the 117th Infantry Brigade on the Left and the 116th Infantry Brigade on the Right. The 16th Battalion SHERWOOD FORESTERS and 17th Battalion KINGS ROYAL RIFLE CORPS were attached to take and consolidate the first objective whilst the 17th Battalion SHERWOOD FORESTERS and 16th Battalion RIFLE BRIGADE were detailed to capture and consolidate the Second objective.	
	8		There was a Brigade Church parade on the 16th Battalion SHERWOOD FORESTERS Parade Ground at which the Deputy Chaplain General BISHOP GWYNNE CMG gave the address. A Brigade Horse Show was held at HOULLE in the afternoon the following is an extract from Battalion Daily Orders:- "The Commander of Officers desires to congratulate Lieut F.L. HOLMES and the NCOs and men who took part in the Brigade Horse Show. Our Battalion won four FIRST PRIZES two SECOND and one THIRD Prize - a most satisfactory result. Also on this to the Enthusiasm and Pride with which all hands have entered into this work." On total points the Battalion comes out SECOND in the Brigade.	

16th Battalion SHERWOOD FORESTERS

WAR DIARY
or
INTELLIGENCE SUMMARY.

Army Form C. 2118.

Place	Date	Hour	Summary of Events and Information	Remarks and references to Appendices
SERQUES	1917 July/16		Training was carried out in the vicinity of Billets.	
			In the evening a football match was arranged between the 16th Battalion and 17th Battalion SHERWOOD FORESTERS football elevens on our Battalion transport lines. The 17th Battalion officers were invited to tea which was partaken of on the ground.	
			The game which showed confusion resulted in a win for the Battalion - 4 goals to 3.	(1)
	17th		A photograph was taken of all the Battalion officers	(2)
	19th		The Battalion took part in a practice BRIGADE DAWN ATTACK on the training ground	(3)
	20th		Practice trenches at LONGUEBOURNE	(4)
	21st		The Battalion with the whole of the 117th Infantry Brigade proceeded from NOVELLE in Motor Lorries and Motor Buses via ST. OMER ESQUELBECQUE and WORMHOUDT to a point about two miles from POPERINGHE on the POPERINGHE - PROVEN road. From here the Battalion proceeded by march route to bivouacs in A.29 (Sheet 28. N.W.) near BRANDHOEK.	
			On the bus journey a two hours halt was made near WORMHOUDT where the Battalion rested and had tea in a REST CAMP.	(5)

16th Battalion SHERWOOD FORESTERS.

WAR DIARY
or
INTELLIGENCE SUMMARY.

Army Form C. 2118.

Place	Date	Hour	Summary of Events and Information	Remarks and references to Appendices
SERQUES	July 21st		The journey was completed by 3.0 am on the 22nd	
	22nd		The Battalion rested	
			At 6.30 pm a Voluntary Church Service was held at which the Rev J F BROXHAM officiated for the first time	
	23 to 27th		Bivouac camp	

WAR DIARY
or
INTELLIGENCE SUMMARY.

Army Form C. 2118.

(Erase heading not required.)

Place	Date	Hour	Summary of Events and Information	Remarks and references to Appendices
NEAR BRANDHOEK	July 28		The Battalion moved into the HILL TOP SECTOR relieving the 6th Batt LINCOLNSHIRE REGT. A.Coy in the front line	
HILL TOP SECTOR			B Coy in support at LA BELLE ALLIANCE, C and D COYS on the CANAL BANK - Battalion Headquarters in the HILL TOP Dugout.	(9)A
	30th		The Battalion assembled in our front line trenches to assault the German trench taphures. This front line captures. A.Coy on the right front and B.Coy on the left front were detailed to capture & consolidate the German front (red) support (yellow) lines whilst C.Coy on the right & D.Coy on the left proceed through & went forward to capture & consolidate the German Reserve line (Blue & Brittle Blue line)	
			The 11th Batt: ROYAL SUSSEX REGT were on our right & the 19th Batt: KINGS ROYAL RIFLE CORPS on our left.	(9)A
	31st		At 3.50 am the artillery barrage opened & our four lines advanced to get as close under it as possible. When followed closely the objectives assigned to the Battalion were secured with little difficulty by A.Coy commanded by CAPT. C.G.LORD, B.Coy commanded	

Army Form C. 2118.

WAR DIARY
or
INTELLIGENCE SUMMARY.
(Erase heading not required.)

Instructions regarding War Diaries and Intelligence
Summaries are contained in F. S. Regs., Part II.
and the Staff Manual respectively. Title pages
will be prepared in manuscript.

Place	Date	Hour	Summary of Events and Information	Remarks and references to Appendices
	July			
HILLTOP	31st		"B" by Capt. P.H. COLERIDGE M.C., C.Coy Commanded by Capt. L.H. ASKWITH and D.Coy commanded by Lieut. T.E.O. WILLIAMS.	
			The enemy held these trenches lightly & only put up a weak resistance. During the advance the Battalion captured 120 Prisoners & 2 Machine Guns. Advanced Battalion Headquarters were established in CAMPHOR TRENCH (were line) and the Consolidation of the Battle Blue Line Commenced. At 8.0 am A.Coy was withdrawn for work under the 227th Field Coy R.E. for road construction.	
			During the day the greater part of the Battalion was employed in carrying forward the Brigade Dump and carrying forward S.A.A. Bombs wire &water to the 17th Batt. SHERWOOD FORESTERS and 16th (S) Batt. RIFLE BRIGADE who had captured KITCHENER'S WOOD and the trench system up to the RIVER STEENBEEK.	
			At 4.30 pm C Coy was sent up to reinforce the 17KRB with the Battalion SHERWOOD FORESTERS and came under the command of the O.C. that Battalion.	

Army Form C. 2118.

WAR DIARY
or
INTELLIGENCE SUMMARY.
(Erase heading not required.)

Place	Date	Hour	Summary of Events and Information	Remarks and references to Appendices
HILL 10P.	July. 31(cont'd)		One platoon of this Company was sent forward to the line of the RIVER STEENBEEK. About 9.0 p.m. B. Coy. was similarly sent up to reinforce this line. 2/Lt A.B. MELLOR was wounded whilst conducting a carrying party to KITCHENER'S WOOD.	

Woolhough? Lt.
Commanding.
11th Batt: SHERWOOD FORESTERS.

11.8.17.

SECRET.

16th Battalion SHERWOOD FORESTERS.
OPERATION ORDER No. 30.

JULY, 24th 1917.

REFERENCE:- ST JULIAN 1/10,000 MAP.
and TRENCH MAPS.

GENERAL OBJECTIVE

1. The Fifth Army is to capture the hostile trench systems EAST and NORTH-EAST of YPRES on "Z" Day.

TASK OF THE BRIGADE.

2. (a) The 117th Infantry Brigade will be the left Brigade of the 39th Division. The 116th Infantry Brigade will be on the right of the Brigade and the 152nd Infantry Brigade (51st Division) on the left of the Brigade.
  (b) The tasks allotted to the Brigade are:-
    (i) To capture the German Front Line System.
    (ii) To capture the KITCHENER System.
    (iii) To secure the crossings of the STEENBEEK.
  (c) The 118th Infantry Brigade will pass through the Brigade at ZERO plus 6 hours 20 minutes and capture the LANGEMARK System.

PLAN OF ATTACK.

3. (a) (i) The 16th Bn Sherwood Foresters on the Right, and the 17th K.R.Rif.C. on the Left will capture the German Front Line System.
    (ii) The 17th Bn Sherwood Foresters on the Right & the 11th Rifle Brigade on the Left will capture the KITCHENER System, and secure the crossings over the STEENBEEK.
  (b) Each Battalion will attack on a two-company frontage, and each Company on a two platoon frontage.
  (c) Detailed objectives and boundaries are shewn on the attached map.
  (d) The advance will be carried out in accordance with the attached Time Table.

4. The Battalion will attack as follows:-
  (a) "A" Company on the right, "B" Company on the left, will form the first two waves, and will capture the RED and YELLOW Lines.
  "C" Company on the right, "D" Company on the left, will form the third & fourth waves, and will capture the BLUE LINE, and make good the DOTTED BLUE LINE, including CAMPHOR SUPPORT.
  (b) The first wave will capture the RED LINE, and the second wave the YELLOW LINE. The third and fourth waves will pass through the first and second waves and capture the BLUE LINE.
  (c) Officer Commanding "A" Company will detail two sections to capture HAMPSHIRE FARM.
  Officer Commanding "D" Company will detail two sections to capture KULTUR FARM.
  These bodies will not continue the advance until the farms have been cleared of the enemy.

REORGANISATION

5. After the capture of the BLACK LINE:-
  (a) The Battalion will reorganise into Brigade Reserve, sending officers and N.C.O's forward to reconnoitre the approaches to the DOTTED BLACK LINE.

CONTINUED......

5. (b) Officer Commanding "B" Company will send back two Platoons to carry forward the Brigade Dump from BELLINGHAM TRENCH to KULTUR FARM.

(c) "A" Company will report to MAJOR HAMMOND 225 Coy R.E. at HAMPSHIRE FARM at ZERO plus 2 hours for construction of roads for the artillery. One shovel per man will be taken.

ASSEMBLY.

6. (a) The first and second waves will assemble in HORNBY TRENCH, the third and fourth waves in FORWARD TRENCH.

(b) Assembly will be complete by ZERO minus 3 hours. Companies to be EAST of BILGE TR. by 11 pm on "Y" day.

(c) Companies will move to their assembly positions by platoons and use overland tracks as far as junction FINCH STREET and BUFFS ROAD.

(d) All lines will advance at ZERO, and will close up under the barrage to enable rear lines to be clear of our line before the enemy barrage becomes intense.

(e) Officers Commanding Companies will arrange for a hot meal to be issued to their men at ZERO minus 2 hours.

(f) Officers Commanding "A" & "B" Companies will be responsible for clearing the wire in front of HORNBY TRENCH, & Officers Commanding "C" & "D" Companies in front of FORWARD TRENCH on "Y" night.

(g) Assembly complete will be reported in writing to Battalion Headquarters by runner.

MACHINE GUNS.

7. One Section 117th Machine Gun Company will go forward with the 4th Wave for the defence of the BLUE LINE.
Two Sections will carry out Machine Gun Barrage under Divisional Orders.

TRENCH MORTARS.

8. (a) One Section 117th Trench Mortar Battery will accompany the second wave and will take up position in the enemy front line, ready to support the advance to the BLUE LINE.
One Section will accompany the fourth wave and take up position in the BLUE LINE to cover consolidation.

ARTILLERY.

9. (a) The rate of the barrage throughout will be 100 yards in 4 minutes.

(b) The various lifts are shown in the attached time table & barrage map. An Artillery F.O.O. will accompany the Battalion. Officers will give him all possible assistance in the maintenance of communications and in the provision of shelter for his personnel.

3

TANKS

10 (a) Four Tanks will work on the Brigade Front. The task allotted to them is the destruction of the BLACK LINE. They will cross the DOTTED BLUE LINE at ZERO plus 1 hour 15 minutes.

(b) These Tanks will accompany the Infantry in the advance to the DOTTED GREEN LINE and cross the STEENBEEK.

(c) The approximate routes to be followed are shown on the attached map.

(d) The details of Tank Employment and co-operation with Infantry, will be issued separately (Instruction no. 7.)

DRESS

11. Fighting Order.

Every man will carry the following:-
1 pair of socks.
Towel & Soap.
Canteen
One complete day's rations
Iron ration
Water-proof Sheet.
Box Respirator (in the alert position)
P.H. Helmet. (The best method is to carry this over the shoulder and under the belt without crossing the chest)
1 Waterbottle (filled) (Two if desired)
Haversack
Entrenching Tool.
4 Sandbags.
2 Mills Grenades } Except Runners, M.G. Coy
2 Flares } and T. Mortar Battery

LIAISON

12. Lieut A.D. PARKIN will report to BRIGADE HEADQUARTERS at HILL TOP as Liaison Officer at ZERO minus 2 hours.

CONTACT PATROL

13 (a) A Contact Patrol will be in the air throughout the attack.

(b) Flares will be lit by leading troops only when called for by the aeroplane.

(c) If leading troops are without flares and are halted, they will wave their helmets to attract the attention of the aeroplane should it call for flares.

COMMUNICATIONS.

14. Brigade Forward Stations will be established as follows:-
1 at KULTUR FARM
2 at OBLONG FARM
3 at ALBERTA

4.

CONTINUED......

14/ Two circuits from Battle Head, one for Infantry, and one for artillery will be laid and maintained to these forward stations.

Lieut C.E. GARLAND will be in charge of the advanced Battalion Command Post, and will accompany the fourth wave, and will establish Battalion Headquarters in CALF RESERVE, about C.16.c.8.5.

HEADQUARTERS.

15/ Headquarters will be as follows from "Y/Z" night.

BRIGADE HEADQUARTERS — HILL TOP TUNNELS Dugout 20, moving forward to OBLONG FARM.

BATTALION HEADQUARTERS — C.21.6.4.2. Junction of BILGE and CONEY Street moving forward to CALF RESERVE about C.16.c.8.5.

SYNCHRONISATION.

16/ One Officer per Company will report to Battalion Headquarters with signal watch to synchronize:—
July 25th & 26th at 7 p.m.
July 27th at 8.30 p.m. & 2 a.m. July 28th.

TRAFFIC.

17/ All Traffic will be by.

IN
CONEY STREET.
CLARK STREET.

OUT.
GILLSON STREET.
FINCH STREET.

Runners will be allowed to use any trench at any time.

MEDICAL

18. The R.A.P., will be at JUNC. of BILGE TRENCH — GILLSON STREET.
Four Stretchers and Six Stretcher Bearers will accompany each Company.
8 Stretchers and 8 Stretcher Bearers will be in reserve in FORWARD TRENCH.
~~Prisoners will be utilized as Stretcher Bearers~~

POLICE.

19. Battle Police will be detailed as follows.

3 men at JUNC. CONEY ST. & BILGE.

Orders will be issued in writing.

5.

CONTINUED........ 19. Officer Commanding "B" Company will establish Stragglers Posts in the German Front Line.

"Y" DAY   20. "Y" Day will be a day of silence throughout the Brigade.

21. ACKNOWLEDGE.

Whitly Captain
Adjutant 16th Bn Sherwood Foresters.

SECRET.

TIME TABLE

BARRAGE.

	ZERO.	ZERO PLUS 6.	ZERO PLUS 18.	ZERO PLUS 26	ZERO PLUS 26 TO ZERO PLUS 1hr 23 mins	ZERO PLUS 1hr 23 mins
	Open on German front line	Lifts from German front line	Lifts from BLUE LINE.	Lifts from DOTTED BLUE LINE.	Protective Barrage in front of DOTTED BLUE LINE.	Protective Barrage lifts.
HORNBY TRENCH.		First line advance barrage lifts	Two subsequent barrage lifts BLUE LINE.	Rear wave arrives at DOTTED BLUE LINE	Consolidating BLUE LINE & Posts in DOTTED BLUE LINE	Unchanged.
	ZERO PLUS 1hr 47 mins	ZERO PLUS 2hrs 3 mins	ZERO PLUS 3hr 40 mins	ZERO PLUS 4hr 5 mins	ZERO PLUS 4hr 13 mins	ZERO PLUS 6hr 28 mins.
BLACK LINE	Continues thinning rate at normal rate	Protective Barrage Open	Protective Barrage lifts	Continues at normal rate	Lifts to Protective Barrage line.	Protective Barrage lifts. 118th Infantry Brigade has passed Brigade.
Unchanged	Reorganisation begins, bringing up barrage, return etc					

16th Bn. SHERWOOD FORESTERS

WAR DIARY
or
INTELLIGENCE SUMMARY.
(Erase heading not required.)

Army Form C. 2118.

Place	Date 1917	Hour	Summary of Events and Information	Remarks and references to Appendices
ST JULIEN	Aug 1st			
	2nd	About 10 pm orders were received for the 111th Infantry Brigade to take over the Divisional front.	
			The 16th Battalion SHERWOOD FORESTERS relieved the 13th Battalion ROYAL SUSSEX REGT. in and behind ST. JULIEN - the night of the Brigade front. Dispositions were :-	
			"D" Company ST JULIEN	
			"C" " CANTEEN & CANOPUS TRENCH.	
			"A" " } DUGOUT IN BETWEEN CANOPUS TR.	
			"B" " AND VENHEULLE FARM	
			Battalion Headquarters - VENHEULLE FARM	
			Relief was completed by 9.30 pm	
			During the process of the Relief, a high velocity shell entered VENHEULLE FARM, killing and injuring 30 other Ranks, including three officers.	
			During the day - Capt L. H. ASKWITH - WOUNDED	
			During Relief - Capt C. H. L. RIXON - SHELLSHOCK	

Army Form C. 2118.

WAR DIARY
or
INTELLIGENCE SUMMARY.
(Erase heading not required.)

Instructions regarding War Diaries and Intelligence Summaries are contained in F. S. Regs., Part II, and the Staff Manual respectively. Title pages will be prepared in manuscript.

Place	Date Aug.	Hour	Summary of Events and Information	Remarks and references to Appendices
	3rd		"A" and "B" Companies were heavily shelled in their dugout positions and suffered heavy casualties. Their positions became untenable and at 6.0 p.m. "A" Company had to withdraw to CAMPHOR TRENCH and "B" Company to CALIFORNIA DRIVE. 2 Platoons of "B" Company were sent up to reinforce the ST JULIEN defences.	
	4th		The enemy bombarded our positions steadily the whole day, and at night placed a heavy barrage on CANTEEN TRENCH, VENHEULLE FARM and the approaches to ST JULIEN. "D" Company accounted for an enemy patrol approaching ST JULIEN from the NORTH. They left five dead on the ground.	
	5th		"D" Company at ST JULIEN again accounted for five of the enemy, and rifled the Village clear of the enemy. A steady bombardment of the defences was kept up making the matter of supplies a great difficulty. At 11.20 p.m. the Battalion was relieved by the 1/5th GLOSTER REGIMENT and proceeded to dugouts on the CANAL BANK.	

WAR DIARY
or
INTELLIGENCE SUMMARY.

Army Form C. 2118.

Place	Date	Hour	Summary of Events and Information	Remarks and references to Appendices
	5th		Owing to a frequent lull of the enemy shelling the relief was carried out steadily and with few casualties. Three enemy guns were found in addition to those taken over from its 13th Battalion ROYAL SUSSEX REGIMENT. Captain P.H. COLERIDGE, M.C., wounded. During this period the very wet weather made the work of holding the line a matter of great difficulty. The dugouts and trenches were very wet during the whole air change, and the men were all wet through and unable to lie down to rest. Rations were brought up nightly on pack animals as far as JEDDAR VILLA in spite of intense shelling. The conduct of all ranks, both during the assault and subsequent transport the trying period subsequent was beyond all praise.	(3)
	6th		The Battalion rested at CANAL BANK. The 39th Division was transferred back to the XIth CORPS, 2nd Army.	(4)
	7th	At 5.50 a.m.	the Battalion proceeded by route march to VLAMERTINGHE	

Army Form C. 2118.

WAR DIARY
or
INTELLIGENCE SUMMARY.
(Erase heading not required.)

Instructions regarding War Diaries and Intelligence Summaries are contained in F. S. Regs., Part II. and the Staff Manual respectively. Title pages will be prepared in manuscript.

Place	Date Aug	Hour	Summary of Events and Information	Remarks and references to Appendices
	7th		STATION, where, at 7.30 p.m. the whole Brigade entrained and proceeded to CAESTRE between CASSEL and BAILLEUL, from here the Battalion	
La Coq de Paille			was taken in Motor Buses to LA COQ de PAILLE where the Battalion was billeted. "A" and "B" Companies in farm buildings, the remainder in Tents. Lieut. Colonel C. HERBERT STEPNEY, D.S.O, mentioned in London Gazette for "Valuable services rendered in connection with the War at home."	
	8th		The General Officer Commanding 39th Division, Major General G.I. CUTHBERT, C.B., C.M.G., addressed the 117th Brigade who were paraded en masse for the purpose. He heartily congratulated the Brigade on its excellent behaviour in the recent operations, in not only capturing all its objectives, but also in keeping a firm hold of them, although counter attacked and very heavily shelled. He said the 39th Division had done best in the whole Army, but in number of prisoners - over one thousand - and in capturing and holding all objectives, also the excellent spirit which all ranks had worked during the very trying time subsequent to	

WAR DIARY
or
INTELLIGENCE SUMMARY.
(Erase heading not required.)

Army Form C. 2118.

Place	Date Aug	Hour	Summary of Events and Information	Remarks and references to Appendices
	9th		the attack. Brigadier General C.A. ARMYTAGE, D.S.O., also heartily congratulated his Brigade and said "As Commander of the 117th Brigade he was the proudest man in the Army".	
	10th		The whole of the 117th Infantry Brigade was inspected by General Sir H.C.O. PLUMER, G.C.M.G., K.C.B., A.D.C., who was attended by the CORPS and DIVISIONAL COMMANDERS.	
	12th		CHURCH PARADE	
	13th		The Battalion entrained at FLETRE and was taken to RIDGE WOOD CAMP immediately South of DICKEBUSCHE LAKE. Here the Battalion was accommodated in tents and dugouts.	
	14th		The Battalion less "A" Company, relieved the 21st Battalion KING'S ROYAL RIFLE CORPS in the front line – KLEIN ZILLEBEKE SECTOR.	

WAR DIARY
or
INTELLIGENCE SUMMARY.

Army Form C. 2118.

Place	Date	Hour	Summary of Events and Information	Remarks and references to Appendices
	14th Aug		"C" and "D" Companies right and left front respectively, "B" Company 1 platoon right, and 1 platoon left Supports, with two platoons at THE CATERPILLAR. Battalion Headquarters in the RAILWAY CUTTING under HILL 60.	
			"A" Company with details from the other Companies proceeded to CARNARVON CAMP under the command of CAPTAIN C.G. LOAD.	
	15th		"D" Company was raided by the enemy:- The Company was "Standing to" rather later than usual on account of the mist, but it was quite light. The enemy advanced in two waves at 20 paces distance through a body 2 which ran 40 yards in front of and parallel to the front line. The attack was preceded by a light barrage of Rifle Grenades and Light Trench Mortars, which fell South of the point selected for entry. It is thought that the enemy was of opinion that we did not occupy the point chosen for attack.	

Army Form C. 2118.

WAR DIARY
or
INTELLIGENCE SUMMARY.
(Erase heading not required.)

Instructions regarding War Diaries and Intelligence Summaries are contained in F. S. Regs., Part II. and the Staff Manual respectively. Title pages will be prepared in manuscript.

Place	Date	Hour	Summary of Events and Information	Remarks and references to Appendices
	Aug 15th		The raiding party advanced shouting & throwing bombs, but were covered through the hedge, met with steady fire from Rifles & Lewis Guns from the garrison - the 16 Platoon. 2nd Lieut A.S. MELLOR and his orderly went out along a Sap on the flank of the raiding party and bombed them with German Grenades, which had been left in their captured dugouts by their previous occupants. 2nd Lieut MELLOR was wounded whilst doing this. C.S.M. BULLIMORE organised and helped to man a Snyping Post on the left of COMPANY HEADQUARTERS. This post accounted for 5 Germans. CAPTAIN R.L. ILLINGWORTH, M.C., and his orderly went down the Sap, and seeing 3 Germans in a shell hole, went for them, and brought them in. Lieut T.C.O. WILLIAMS, and two other ranks went to bring in a man who appeared to be wounded. He brought him in and seeing	

WAR DIARY
or
INTELLIGENCE SUMMARY.

(Erase heading not required.)

Army Form C. 2118.

Place	Date	Hour	Summary of Events and Information	Remarks and references to Appendices
	15th		six others in a shell hole, brought them in also Lance Corporal HURT, who had previously been cut with Lieut WILLIAMS, then went out again & brought in a further party of four. A patrol went out at dusk to look for wounded. It found no wounded but counted 20 bodies of dead Germans. There were other bodies visible, but it was found impossible to count them as they were to near a German Post. The net result of the raid was:- 13 unwounded prisoners. 1 wounded (since died) from 20 to 25 killed. Our casualties:- 2nd Lt. A.S. MELLOR & one other Rank - wounded later in the day, the Commanding Officer was wounded in its left arm by a sniper whilst proceeding to "D" Company Headquarters to convey to CAPTAIN R.L. ILLINGWORTH, M.C. the congratulations of the Army	

WAR DIARY
or
INTELLIGENCE SUMMARY.

Army Form C. 2118.

(Erase heading not required.)

Instructions regarding War Diaries and Intelligence Summaries are contained in F. S. Regs., Part II. and the Staff Manual respectively. Title pages will be prepared in manuscript.

Place	Date Aug	Hour	Summary of Events and Information	Remarks and references to Appendices
	15th		Remainder of so successfully mopping up the enemy raid	
	17th		The Battalion was relieved by the 17th Battalion SHERWOOD FORESTERS, and proceeded to SUPPORT – One Company and Battalion Headquarters in the old German front and Support trenches, and the two other Companies in the O.B.L. (THE RAVINE)	
	19th		Two Companies were sent up to dig a new Support trench at KLEIN ZILLEBEKE	
RIDGE WOOD	20th		The Battalion was relieved by the 4/5th BLACK WATCH and proceeded to RIDGEWOOD CAMP.	
			MAJOR N. HOUGHTON assumed Command of the Battalion vice LIEUT. COLONEL STEPNEY, D.S.O. Appointed COMMANDING OFFICER, vice CAPTAIN R. L. ILLINGWORTH, M.C., appointed Acting Second-in-Command	

WAR DIARY
or
INTELLIGENCE SUMMARY.
(Erase heading not required.)

Army Form C. 2118.

Place	Date	Hour	Summary of Events and Information	Remarks and references to Appendices
	1917 Aug			
	20th		CAPTAIN A. STEVENSON. M.C. placed in Temporary command of "D" Company	
			MAJOR GENERAL E. FEETHAM. C.B., C.M.G. assumed command of the 39th Division vice MAJOR GENERAL C.J CUTHBERT C.B., C.M.G., proceeding to ENGLAND to have a Division there	
			The following letter of farewell was received from the MAJOR GENERAL:-	
			"39th Division - I have been ordered to proceed to England, to take up the command of a Division there, and in bidding you farewell, I wish to thank all ranks most sincerely for your unvarying gallantry, good conduct and soldierly spirit which has made the whole period of my command one of intense pride and pleasure. You have never failed to give of your best willingly, cheerfully and fully, either when training in billets or when holding the line. Rest you have never known, but your good spirit and great fighting qualities have successfully carried you through all fatigue, dangers & difficulties.	

WAR DIARY
or
INTELLIGENCE SUMMARY.

(Erase heading not required.)

Army Form C. 2118.

Place	Date	Hour	Summary of Events and Information	Remarks and references to Appendices
	Aug. 20th		Memories of your Victories on the ANCRE, at SCHWABEN REDOUBT, at STUFF TRENCH and at ST PIERRE DIVION together with the recent third Battle of YPRES, will always remain my proudest recollection, and I know that in future, as in the past, your one thought will always be for the honour and good name of the Division, and the BLUE and WHITE badge. — GOODBYE.	
	21st		A and "D" Companies were detailed for work under the 224th FIELD COMPANY, R.E.	
	22nd		The following letter was received from Lieut. Colonel C. HERBERT-STEPNEY, D.S.O.:-	
			"AUGUST 20th HOSPITAL, FRANCE. "Please give my best wishes to all Officers & other Ranks of the Battalion and say how much I feel leaving them all. I hope you will continue to good luck you have had	

WAR DIARY
or
INTELLIGENCE SUMMARY.
(Erase heading not required.)

Army Form C. 2118.

Place	Date Aug	Hour	Summary of Events and Information	Remarks and references to Appendices
	22nd		I have got a nasty wound in my left upper arm and left side, and I fear that my soldiering with the Battalion is done. My arm was amputated yesterday near the shoulder.	
HOLLEBEKE	23rd		The Battalion relieved the 12th Sussex Regiment in the HOLLEBEKE RIGHT SUB-SECTION. "A" Company on the left, and "B" Company on the right, being the two front line Companies. "D" Company in Support and "C" Company in Reserve.	
	25th		"A" Company were relieved by "D" Company, and proceeded to the SUPPORT LINES.	
BOIS CONFLUENT	27th		The Battalion was relieved by the 17th Battalion SHERWOOD FORESTERS, and moved to Reserve billets in BOIS CONFLUENT CAMP. During the tour in the trenches the casualties amounted to 10 - Lieut W.T. HASTINGS and 9 OTHER RANKS being wounded.	

Army Form C. 2118.

WAR DIARY
or
INTELLIGENCE SUMMARY.
(Erase heading not required.)

Place	Date Aug	Hour	Summary of Events and Information	Remarks and references to Appendices
	27th		A draft of 5 Sergeants arrived from the Reinforcement Camp	
ONTARIO CAMP	29th		The Battalion was relieved by the 4th MIDDLESEX REGT, and proceeded by route march to ONTARIO CAMP, RENING HELST. The following letter was received from the son of Lieut Colonel C. HERBERT - STEPNEY, D.S.O.:- "I am writing on behalf of my mother, to thank you for your letter. We are staying in Rouen, where my father is at No.2 Red Cross Hospital Army Post Office 2. My father is in a very dangerous state, his left arm is amputated and is very septic. The wound in his chest has healed, but did not damage the lung, and it is clean; the arm is the danger. Four news of the wound is good, but my father is not fit to be spoken to much at present, as we are not giving it to him. I hope you will excuse my Mother not writing, but she is very done up with sitting up with my father, and is now reacting.	

WAR DIARY
or
INTELLIGENCE SUMMARY.
(Erase heading not required.)

Army Form C. 2118.

Place	Date Aug.	Hour	Summary of Events and Information	Remarks and references to Appendices
	29th		We miss try to let you know news of my father as often as we can and no doubt you will let the Battalion hear its report.	
	30th		A Voluntary service was held at which special intercessions were offered on behalf of Lieut Colonel C. HERBERT STEPNEY, D.S.O.	
			24 OTHER RANKS rejoined Battalion from the Base Depot. The following decorations were awarded for gallantry and devotion to duty during the hostile raid on August 15th 1917.	
			BAR TO MILITARY CROSS	
			CAPTAIN R L ILLINGWORTH M.C.	
			MILITARY CROSS	
			2ND LIEUT A.S. MELLOR	

WAR DIARY
or
INTELLIGENCE SUMMARY

Army Form C. 2118.

DISTINGUISHED CONDUCT MEDAL

No.26733 C.S.M. BULLIMORE R. "D" Coy.

BAR TO MILITARY MEDAL

No.20483 Pte. J. ROBINSON "D" Coy.   No.26804 Pte. H. EARNATH "D" Coy.

MILITARY MEDAL

No.26299 L/c MARSH. H. "D" Coy.   No.12821 L/c HURT. S. "D" Coy.

The following N.C.Os and men were awarded the MILITARY MEDAL for gallantry and devotion to duty during the operations July 31st to August 6th 1917.

No.39930 Pte. WILLIAMS. G. "D" Coy.   No.26285. Pte. ELSON. J.H. "C" Coy
" 16556 L/S NEALE. A. "D" "   " 27267 " POXON. W. "A" "
" 27329 Sgt JAYES. J. "C" "   " 25900 L/S COLLEDGE. S. "A" "
" 24184 Pte CORPE. T. "D" "   " 27392 Cpl CHALLIS. A.W. "A" "

Army Form C. 2118.

WAR DIARY
or
INTELLIGENCE SUMMARY.

(Erase heading not required.)

Place	Date	Hour	Summary of Events and Information	Remarks and references to Appendices
			27092 Pte NIGHTINGALE. E "A" Coy No 25810 Pte BARBER.C "A" Coy	
			20458 " HAMBROOK.E "A" " 26148 cpl CRICH.A "B" "	
			26638 Cpl LEAKE.G "D" " 32250 Pte LOVATT.P.C "C" "	
			27395 L/S PACE. R.J "D" " 76275 " BUTCHART.T "B" "	
			71548 Pte TAYLOR.S.A "B" " 26469 Cpl BENNETT.G.W "C" "	
			26670 Sgt BREED.T.C "B" " 24803 Sgt THOMPSON.J. "C" "	
			BAR TO MILITARY MEDAL	
			No.26208. Sgt SHELDON.E. "B" COMPANY	
			A.Houghton Major	
			Commanding 16th Bn Sherwood Foresters	

WAR DIARY or INTELLIGENCE SUMMARY

Army Form C. 2118.

11/39
16 Nth 9 Reedy
Vol 19

Place	Date	Hour	Summary of Events and Information	Remarks and references to Appendices
Ontario Camp	1917 Sept 1st		Church Parade in Camp 10.30 am.	
NEAR			In the Afternoon the Battalion "Football XI" played a match against the 39th Divisional Ammunition Column B Game resulting in a draw both sides scoring twice	AOD
Renninghelst	3rd		Major J. Houghton transferred to the Rank of Acting Lieut Colonel from 16.5.17 whilst commanding the Battalion vice Lieut Colonel C. Robert Stilwell D.S.O. evacuated 15.5.17.	AOO
	4th		The Battalion left Ontario Camp near RENINGHELST after lunch and marched to the	
STEENVOORDE AREA			Captain F.E. Tidy M.C. proceeded on leave to Rouen with E.S. list	RCA
	5th		The following were awarded the Distinguished Conduct Medal for Gallantry and Skill in Action —	
			No 36138 Coy'y Sergt DELVES F. "3" Coy. 76051 L/Corpl EDWARDS "A" Coy. 26887 Sergeant HARDY W. "D" Coy. 47672 Private SLATER A. "B" Coy	

19A
S.D.

Army Form C. 2118.

WAR DIARY
or
INTELLIGENCE SUMMARY.
(Erase heading not required.)

Instructions regarding War Diaries and Intelligence Summaries are contained in F. S. Regs., Part II. and the Staff Manual respectively. Title pages will be prepared in manuscript.

Place	Date	Hour	Summary of Events and Information	Remarks and references to Appendices
	1917			
	5th & 5th		Battalion Training	R.O.
	6th		Battalion Training. The 1st of the Battalion inter Coy Football Competition between B & D Companies took place in the evening. Result B Coy 3 D Coy Nil	R.O.
	7th		Battalion Training. In the afternoon the Battalion sports were held at Headquarters at 2.30 pm	R.O.
	8th		The Battalion took part in Brigade training "Practice of the Assault". Captain J.F.Lilly M.C. returned from leave. Captain G.J.Ford M.C. proceeded on Leave to England.	R.O.
	9th		Church Parade. The G.O.C. addressed the Brigade Parade and the Divisional Commander Brigaded decorations to all Warrant Officers, N.C.O's and men to whom away to that had been granted on and after the 31st July 1917.	R.O.

WAR DIARY
or
INTELLIGENCE SUMMARY.
(Erase heading not required.)

Army Form C. 2118.

Place	Date	Hour	Summary of Events and Information	Remarks and references to Appendices
	1917			
	Sept 9		After the parade Brigade leans were held to shoot how we all Co. the	
			BATTALION SHERWOOD FORESTERS who scored 27 Bands: the Battalion could also	
			win a prize of 24/- Bands	220
		10	The Brigade Brasband then played on the Esprance of the Divisional Commander(s)	
			In the evening a Band of the Sherwood Foresters, the Cambrai Rifles competed for the Rollins	
			between a Combined Band of the 19th "King's" Royal Rifle Corps and 5 Coy of this	
			Battalion. Result - B Coy. 5 Gools. KRRC. 2 Gools.	220
		11-	Captain L.F. Littel M.C. proceeded to England on a months leave	
			In the morning the Battalion practised to Section the assault	
			B Coy. Band of the 12th L.T.M. Battery were tried at the End of the Series but Combined assault	
			Combinations - the result being a return to 1st Coy. of Coy B. Cooks to 1 Gool.	
			The following Honours were awarded the "MILITARY CROSS" for Gallantry on 4 devotion	
			to Duty during the operations July 31st to August 6th 1917.	
			CAPTAIN ASKWITH. L.H. CAPTAIN C6/LORD. CAPTAIN PULLAN.	

WAR DIARY or INTELLIGENCE SUMMARY.

Army Form C. 2118.

(Erase heading not required.)

Place	Date	Hour	Summary of Events and Information	Remarks and references to Appendices
	1917 11.11		LIEUT T.C.O. WILLIAMS. LIEUT W.T. HASTINGS.	
	12th		The Battalion proceeded to MORTH BUSSES to ROSE WOOD CAMP taking over huts from the 4/5th BLACK WATCH after which Herr went to training the Battalion less details proceeded up to the line taking over the Regt. Battalion SHREWSBURY FOREST SECTOR from the 13th BATTALION ROYAL SUSSEX REGIMENT. 2nd LIEUT A. ROBINSON and 3 other Ranks were wounded and 3 other Ranks missing.	
	13th		Shortly after midnight of the 12/13th CAPTAIN C.F. BOWER was Killed and 2nd LIEUT F.G. MORRIS severely wounded - also SERGEANT GYTE A. The Enemy shelled the whole Battalion area all the day. At 10 am the Commanding Officer - LIEUT COLONEL N. HOUGHTON was Killed near Battalion Headquarters - Also SERGEANT PEPPER C. MAJOR T.R. WEBSTER M.C. of 17th BATTALION SHERWOOD FORESTERS was sent to Command the Battalion.	
			Casualties :- 2 Officers Killed, 1 Officer wounded. Other Ranks 1 Killed, 1 Wounded.	

Army Form C. 2118.

WAR DIARY
or
INTELLIGENCE SUMMARY.
(Erase heading not required.)

Instructions regarding War Diaries and Intelligence Summaries are contained in F. S. Regs., Part II. and the Staff Manual respectively. Title pages will be prepared in manuscript.

Place	Date	Hour	Summary of Events and Information	Remarks and references to Appendices
	1917 14th		Visited by the Divisional Commander	No.
	15th		The Battalion was relieved by the 3rd Battalion Royal Sussex Regiment and proceeded to the Busseboom Camp at H.5.d. (Sheet 28) near Ridge Wood. Casualties - O.R. 1 Killed, 4 wounded, 1 missing	No.
	16th, 17th		Whilst at the Busseboom Camp details were sent for to front line trenches	No.
	18th		The Battalion relieved the 13th Battalion Royal Sussex Regiment at ZWARTELEEN Near Hill 60 and became Battalion in Support in the SHREWSBURY FOREST SECTOR. About 120 details were left behind at the Divisional Reinforcement Camp A draft of 61 O.Rs. arrived	No.
	19th		2nd LIEUT. T. W. FLEWITT returned to duty also a draft of 31 O.R. Captain C. G. LORD M.C. returned from leave in England.	No.

D. D. & L., London, E.C.
(A7883) Wt. W807/M1672 350,000 4/17 **Sch. 82a** Forms/C/2118/14

WAR DIARY
or
INTELLIGENCE SUMMARY.

Army Form C. 2118.

(Erase heading not required.)

Instructions regarding War Diaries and Intelligence Summaries are contained in F. S. Regs., Part II. and the Staff Manual respectively. Title pages will be prepared in manuscript.

Place	Date	Hour	Summary of Events and Information	Remarks and references to Appendices
	1917 3/10		SHREWSBURY FOREST:- The Battalion attacked the Enemy line	
	4/10		The assembly was carried out in good order in spite of the darkness of the night and the heavy and very complete enemy Barrage. Before Zero, Whilst on the Assembly positions we were Shelled slightly which caused a few casualties. Enemy Artillery opened 30 seconds after ZERO causing about 20 casualties [illegible] and not a single Gun heard at our Centre Co. Head Qrs. The trouble had been not so much put of a Zero barrage but harassing fire which grew in volume but however with the Rear Wave of the 17th BATTALION SHERWOOD FORESTERS. Several of such we met at the time and the fell hostile means of keeping direction was the use of Compasses. The Centre Company bore off to the left slightly carrying the left Company with them. This however was corrected and the various strengths reorganized by the Company Officers whilst the 17th BATTALION SHERWOOD FORESTERS were consolidating the RED LINE. Throughout the advance we were under Machine Gun and rifle fire but owing to the fog not very heavy. Casualties were caused in the O.C. of the Centre Company	

WAR DIARY
or
INTELLIGENCE SUMMARY
(Erase heading not required.)

Army Form C. 2118.

Place	Date	Hour	Summary of Events and Information	Remarks and references to Appendices
			(CAPTAIN P.E. BURROWS M.C.) went forward to ascertain how where the Gunners Coy. had found itself and that there was no Event. Machine Guns in action at Beech Bank to	
			Burst out to the South of our battalion with a Platoon which sent Guns were 2/M. Skilling in the position two Vickers Gunsmith to his new area (between	
			In the Bug. Sub. the Brigade ordered Walker to establish his new position Headquarters and required and not for	
			At 4 pm our own Aeroplanes and having were attempted to the attack of the Bim LINE. The Line was not much advanced and it was sent back to Bug Out LE WELBECK	
			GRANGE. Lot at L.M. Gun and the guns of Lewis Gun in action the and several Lewis Gunners No. attached on the Blues were finally relieved. Covered	
			M.G. lost by one of the attached Vickers Guns from the 59th Bryces a Body was sent to the L.M. Gun. But the Nature who had my had in North Gillionek	
			Wounded by CORPORAL EGERTON of the support Company during M.G. Fire. It was shot	
			29 Prisoners including Wood and the Machine Gun our Palm Fire Own Gading troops made a Body. Close up to the Barrage and advancing steadily through	
			Mr. Wood. Lent. Lord Abbey. Men was push up to from NORTH FARM the line to be at from	

WAR DIARY
or
INTELLIGENCE SUMMARY.
(Erase heading not required.)

Army Form C. 2118.

Place	Date	Hour	Summary of Events and Information	Remarks and references to Appendices
			2nd Lieut W Corbould. Was a Stretcher with 2nd Lieut G F WHITE at the head when he was hit as there will no advance of the Battalion on either side, but the Battalion on our right the Somers? Staff W Horsh somewhat took up line of the barrage. On the right of the line Capt. Corbould of No. 10 Lancs North Rifle Corps and the Division on our left made Company was short which was having the same amount of Dead, caused to fall back Lieut Cyril (Can-amon) (2nd Lieut W B Winter.) One half the situation and immediately brought his two Guns to the edge of the wood and did obstruct advance from on the East who were with from and got two shots about on the wing of the South Grenade at by the Enemy I tried to help but was caught by two two? J.R.P.	
			Private W S E More of this Battalion who was hardly out of the Snow and listened to his Comrades? Who did have prisoners and taken away by the Enemy Guns were taken by the Royal Rifle Corps large numbers making in all 33 who all was shot brought back of the 2nd Royal Rifle Corps. This aftternoon was close over left flank was able to gradually advance to the Blue Line where Second of the Enemy were taken prisoners from Old? trench and Several killed by Rifle	

WAR DIARY or INTELLIGENCE SUMMARY

Army Form C. 2118.

(Erase heading not required.)

Place	Date	Hour	Summary of Events and Information	Remarks and references to Appendices

There is no telephone to the ground.

We took up a position on the RIDGE LINE at T.26.c.0.2 this was a long trench Dug-out in which the enemy were firing machine Guns lived but it retired immediately [illegible] the attack of the W. Yorks & C.S. 2nd/4 on the left and Gates Coys were immediately ordered to attack the Blue Line the C. and B. Coys went forward being somewhat ahead of the W. Yorks tunnelers were started with bombs [illegible] supports and [illegible] the Coys went forward. After a [illegible] and got into the Dug Outs from which the Bosches in position to Business were sheltering. While C Coy and I passed Master the bosches were shown to [illegible] the W. Yorks Lewis Gun team and a Lewis Gun and I believed disposed of very effectively for being about 70 yards in advance of the Blue Line and although scattered and back eventually were kept short & visible to the BASSEVILLE BEEK.

During the advance 2nd Lieut. BT McPHERSON Commanding one of the platoons of my Baker Company. I [illegible] forward his platoon on his own initiative Capturing some of Corner Dug-Outs about T.26.C.6.8 from which the Bosches were being shelled. Major & and 2 [illegible] Queens taken. The [illegible] the building at the [illegible] [illegible] from where CHATSWORTH CASTLE was [illegible] of a Bosch wireless. RIDGE LINE was Cololated them to all Business is includes of a completed Offices.

2nd LIEUT. H M MEAKIN [illegible]

WAR DIARY
or
INTELLIGENCE SUMMARY
(Erase heading not required.)

Army Form C. 2118.

Place	Date	Hour	Summary of Events and Information	Remarks and references to Appendices
			was killed	
			2nd Lieuts F.N. BEWLEY and F.C. GRAVES were killed during the advance	
			Whilst Consolidation was proceeding in rear under 2nd Lieut APPLE and Mason in G.14 a view but	
			were able to inflict severe casualties on the Enemy. At about 11 a.m. a runner from to N.F.	
			tried to come over but the advance hopeless of the hill.	
			About this time Lieut WC Graham had been hit. Captains CRAWFORD, HOBBINS, CHISHOLM had been	
			hit and it was judged advisable to send for more Bombs + Small arm ammunition. Colonel	
			FOWLER sent for some Captain MULHALL Company of the 19th BATTALION SHERWOOD FORESTERS	
			occupied our B.Coys support of our own Second Line.	
			At about 5.30 p.m. the Enemy were seen to be circulating in the East in rear of the K.S.L.I.	
			between bombs 60.CH and 05. These bombs were subjected to Lewis and Machine Gun fire	
			under the direction of Captain MILLAR. His Consolidation had such to have retired	
			Captain R.F. LEWIS sent a message up ward to the Wiltshires and the ?? had been shelled	
			at 6.55 p.m. the Enemy was shelled our Counter-attack was launched from Company and the ??	
			of the ??? the S.O.S. was immediately put up and the situation of our Artillery	
			and Machine Guns was excellent a very heavy barrage being put along the Enemy	

WAR DIARY or INTELLIGENCE SUMMARY

Army Form C. 2118.

Place	Date	Hour	Summary of Events and Information	Remarks and references to Appendices
			and the Enemy must have had many casualties	
			at 9.45 p.m. and a message was sent to cease all the Barrage and no Bizars were	
			sent. The night passed quietly except for sniping on our Western	
			Gun Fire. Our Snipers gave themselves as having 8 during the night.	100
	21st		At about 9.45 am Snipers reported that the Enemy were observed on the ridge S.W. of TOWER	
			HAMLETS with our Barrage 100 yards in rear of them. The Enemy were seen up to the	
			ridges built and efforts were made to get our Artillery on to this enemy target but our R.A.F.	
			Liaison saw two aircraft on there, when two Vickers Guns of Machine Gun Section the	
			range of 1350 yards but unfortunately all the Shots of the L.M.G. Guns were by Vis-reads on	
			the ridge and to it was impossible to correct the laying of the Guns. Late patrols	
			of our 14ants (Battalion N.E. Durham) were sent to to ascertain if the Consolidated	
			BULGAR WOOD was unoccupied. Battle Orders Zero at 10.40 pm but not until	
			Rear battle had was difficult for Casualties as there was no instructions and the Enemy	
			being well dug in put a Barrage at 10 pm and at 6 pm to S.O.S. with	
			that fire was to be a Battalion on our left. The Enemy had by this new consolidating by not	
			fired from the Battalion on our left.	

WAR DIARY
or
INTELLIGENCE SUMMARY.
(Erase heading not required.)

Army Form C. 2118.

Place	Date	Hour	Summary of Events and Information	Remarks and references to Appendices
Curragh Camp	23rd		Observers and agents at work. Have hitherto reported 46 enemy casualties. Mr. B. Hahn took 1 tank, 200 knives & 4 Richard-Young rifle knife. Remainder authorized bodies and equipment. In the evening the Battalion was joined by the HERBERT'S REGIMENT 5th Infantry. Details through Depot of the Sussex Regt. and Sussex to serve as Guards men who were not to suit acquainted with the ultimate knots of the Battalion ready action. Known as Woods. LIEUT. F.P. HOLMES (Transport Officer) was authorised/authorized unable taking a Camp on commissioned to the line. Mr. W. Coley the Welsh Herald R.R. BRASSERIE and Corporal S. Bearson the CURRAGH CAMP near WESTHOUTRE. Cable A. Simmons M.C. was wounded during the Kelly. Total Casualties. 2 officers killed, 2 officers wounded. Other Ranks 36 Killed. 136 Wounded and M.M. missing. Col. of Work Gen. 11th Infantry Brigade.	

WAR DIARY
or
INTELLIGENCE SUMMARY.
(Erase heading not required.)

Army Form C. 2118.

Place	Date	Hour	Summary of Events and Information	Remarks and references to Appendices
			" Major General Commander to see Brigade & the Cwf of Commands & here a to Camp to see Units of the Division to observation by the march, whilst the Division Carried out Field Operations as on the 20th September 1915" Copy of Wire sent 11 1/5 instant to CO reports "Letter & Telegram received from Brigade Commanders Congratulating all Staff and other Units & the Corps Commander for the great Service they have rendered & & tendering the message to the Brigadier wishes to Congratulate and thank all Ranks for the welcome present by 2nd Yesterday	
	25th		The Battalion moved by Motor Bus to RIDGE WOOD CAMP near BRASSERIE 25 hrs attached to 227th Company R.E. 50 hrs attached A.D.M.S. 19th Division as Stretcher Bearers LIEUT O.E. GARLAND and 2nd LIEUT H.M. MEAKIN proceeded on leave to England	
RIDGE WOOD	26th		63 Men attached to 13th Field Ambulance as workers / Stretcher Bearers	

Army Form C. 2118.

WAR DIARY
or
INTELLIGENCE SUMMARY.
(Erase heading not required.)

Instructions regarding War Diaries and Intelligence Summaries are contained in F. S. Regs., Part II. and the Staff Manual respectively. Title pages will be prepared in manuscript.

Place	Date	Hour	Summary of Events and Information	Remarks and references to Appendices
WAKEFIELD HUTS CAMP NEAR ROURE	27th		2nd Lieut. B.F. McPherson proceeded on leave to England	NA
			7th Battalion strength of March 1917 = 6 Wakefield Huts Camp near Roure	
			Captain I.T.B. Harrison reporting for duty	
	28th		Abnormal casualties of auxiliary horses reason 11 horses & 1 mule	NA
	29th		2nd Lieut. W.E. Wright proceeded to the General Instrument School	NA
	30th		The G.O.C. 39th Divisional Train Lieut. E. Fretton C.B. ceased to be attached to this unit & proceeded on duty to England	
			1st Wakefield Hut Camp was transferred to Roure Depot & 9th Battalion A Brigade marched to Roure Camp & was taken on strength for rations (Bugle Wood) on the 20th Oct & on ?	
			9 General Archives attached to O.H.R.S. Wakefield Huts Camp for rations	NA
			Casualties	

B. Webster Major
Commanding 7th Battalion Middlesex Regt

Army Form C. 2118.

WAR DIARY
or
INTELLIGENCE SUMMARY.

(Erase heading not required.)

OCTOBER 1917 1/7th Sherwood Foresters

Place	Date	Hour	Summary of Events and Information	Remarks and references to Appendices
WAKEFIELD HUTS (near LOCRE)	1st		Major R.L.ILLINGWORTH M.C. proceeded to the IX Corps Rifle is not Camp to take command of the Reinforcements to Bn. Hd. 117th Infantry Brigade.	
	2nd		The Battalion Football XI played the 1st XI of the 1/7th Sherwood Foresters. Winning - 1 goal to Nil.	
	3rd		Inter Company Sporting Competitions were held on the Range. The following athletics events took place - A Coy #3.5 B Coy #0.2 D Coy were unable to attend - C Coy #3.5. Special thanks to the weather was also.	
	4.17		M/Major H.A.LEGGETT rejoined the Battalion from 1/0 2nd Divisional Camp STAPLES. 2nd/Lt G. SABIN's invalided to England (27.9.17)	
	5.17		Major H.A.LEGGETT returned Major R.ILLINGWORTH M.C. at the IX Corps Reinforcement Camp	20A

Army Form C. 2118.

WAR DIARY (Battalion)
or
INTELLIGENCE SUMMARY.

(Erase heading not required.)

Instructions regarding War Diaries and Intelligence Summaries are contained in F. S. Regs., Part II. and the Staff Manual respectively. Title pages will be prepared in manuscript.

Place	Date	Hour	Summary of Events and Information	Remarks and references to Appendices
	6.1.17		Major J.R. WEBSTER M.C. promoted to Lt-Col., of Kishikishini	
			2nd Lts R.C. DAVIES M.C., W.H.L. BULFIELD and J. SABINE from one	
			Lieut F.R. HOLMES arrived at A SIMELRO M.S. invalided to England.	A
	7.1.17		Capt. Paroli Major R.L. TUNWORTH returned from IX Corps Reinforcement Camp	
			A draft of 100 Other Ranks arrived.	A
	8.1.17		The Battalion was inspected whilst in training by the Divisional Commander.	
			A draft of 14 Other Ranks arrived.	A
	9.1.17		Battalion Route March.	A
	11.1.17		The Battalion was inspected whilst in training by the Divisional Commander.	
			2/Lieuts. B.C.B. WILES and and H.B. BUSWELL reported for duty and	
			were posted to B and D Coys respectively.	
			Lieut. Col. C. HERBERT STEPNEY, D.S.O. invalided to England.	A

WAR DIARY
or
INTELLIGENCE SUMMARY.

(Erase heading not required.)

Army Form C. 2118.

Instructions regarding War Diaries and Intelligence Summaries are contained in F. S. Regs., Part II. and the Staff Manual respectively. Title pages will be prepared in manuscript.

Place	Date	Hour	Summary of Events and Information	Remarks and references to Appendices
	12th		Battalion route march. "C" Coy R.A.F. aircraft as 3 R.F. informant.	
			Dr Battalion 2nd XI played the 2nd XI of the 17th Bn. SHERWOODS	
			FORESTERS. Losing 3 goals - 1 goal.	
			Capt C.G. LORD M.C. proceeded to 6 IX Corps Reinforcement Camp to L.B.	
			to command of the Battalion on returning Reinforcements him.	(4)
	13th		Capt S.F. LILLEY M.C. returned from a month's leave in England.	
			The Battalion 1st XI played the 1st XI of the 17th Bn. SHERWOOD FORESTERS	
			at football winning – 6 goals to 3.	(5)
			Revd. W.H.H. BULKELEY took over the command of A Coy.	
	14th		The following Other Ranks received Cards of Appreciation from the	
			Divisional Commander for Gallantry during the operations on	(4)
			Sept 20th and 21st.	
			632.8. C.S.M. COKAYNE A. 57076. C.S.M. ARKINSTALL N. 20342. Sergt. WALKER B. 26/134 Sgt 4	
			NUSSETTA 26274 Sergt FREER A. 26731 Sergt WILSON E.A. 27504 Corp. MOSS W.I.	

A6945 Wt. W11422/M1160 350,000 12/16 D. D. & L. Forms/C/2118/14.

WAR DIARY or INTELLIGENCE SUMMARY

Army Form C. 2118.

Place	Date	Hour	Summary of Events and Information	Remarks and references to Appendices
	14th (cont.)		26177 L/Cpl. WALKER F.H. 7138 Cpl EGERTON E. 3917 Cpl GILLATT E. 16802 L/Cpl HANES J.	
			32356 L/Cpl PRICE H.E. 16491 L/Cpl SARGERSON J. 26235 L/Cpl ELSON G.H. 26183 L/Cpl MILLSON H.	
			16458 Pte ADAMS F. 50363 Pte BAINES J. 13406 Pte BAXTER G.A. 15629 Pte BELL J. 71105 Pte BECKETT W.	
			50580 Pte COOPER E. 51679 Pte COOPER R. 53405 Pte GOLD W. 71611 Pte BROTHERS H.	
			20458 Pte HAWBROOK A. 31089 Pte HOLLINS D. 25713 Pte ISAAC T.F. 2122 Pte LEES W.	
			51830 Pte LISSANDRE S. 24659 Pte MARTIN R. 7132 Pte FORFAR R.R. 26290 Pte PARDOE W. 54363 Pte RICHARDSON N.	
			2124 Pte SMITH G. 22602 Pte THORNLEY B. 41832 Pte WILKINSON A.T.	
	15th		Battalion marched from Wakefield Huts Camp to Dead Dog Farm Bivouacs.	
			Camp near RIBAE-WOOD.	
	16th		The 39th Division handed over to the XIth Corps. Day Quiet.	
	17th		Inter platoon football.	

WAR DIARY
or
INTELLIGENCE SUMMARY.
(Erase heading not required.)

Army Form C. 2118.

Instructions regarding War Diaries and Intelligence Summaries are contained in F. S. Regs. Part II. and the Staff Manual respectively. Title pages will be prepared in manuscript.

Place	Date	Hour	Summary of Events and Information	Remarks and references to Appendices
	18th		2nd Lieut F.W.M. March was placed tempy i/c 117 Bn Machine Gun Brigade and the 118th Machine Gun Brigade. 2nd Lieut Winnington 26 Bomb — Nob. The Officers for No 117 & 118 Brigade were – Capt Leake 16.23, Lt Hoskine KRRC, Capt Whitby M.G.C., Lt White 16.S.F., Cpl Page Staffords, Major Burrows 16.S.F., C.Q.M.S. Radford Royal Fus. Capt. Dodson KRRC., Capt. Hall Royal Hus, W.O.I Webster 16.S.F., Lt Valentine M.G.C. Capt Collins 17.S.F., Capt. Harrison 16.S.F., Capt. Brown KRRC. A new Draft of 82 Other Ranks arrived.	
	19th		Lieut F. H. Gosling and 2nd Lieut W. E. Wright proceeded on leave to England. The Battalion was A Coy. relieved the 13th & 15th Bn Royal Sussex Regt on the left front. Tower Hamlet sector. B Coy on the right front. C Coy in the left front and D Coy in Support. A Coy moved Lieut W.H.L. Bulkeley was left in/chrg at Voormezeele and was used for carrying parties to the front line. Casualties — 3 killed. 12 wounded.	

WAR DIARY
or
INTELLIGENCE SUMMARY.
(Erase heading not required.)

Army Form C. 2118.

Place	Date	Hour	Summary of Events and Information	Remarks and references to Appendices
	20th		The enemy shelled our Support Area with 5.9"s and 4.2s	
			Casualties - 9 wounded.	(1)
	21st		Visited by the Divisional Commander.	
			Casualties - 6 wounded.	(1)
	22nd	5.0am	At 5.0am the Headquarters Dugout was set alight by the Medical Corporal Pouring Paraffin into the Brazier instead of water, whilst preparing hot tea. In a few seconds the whole place was a sheet of flames, and the issue only gave time to get everyone out. Sergt. C.S.E. the Battalion Signals Sergt. behaved in a most gallant manner. He rushed into the dugout and pulled out an unconscious man. All the material in the dugout was burnt. A new Headquarters had to be established in the vicinity.	(1)
			Lieut. A.D.PARKIN — wounded. O.R's 1 Killed. 3. wounded	

WAR DIARY
or
INTELLIGENCE SUMMARY

Army Form C. 2118.

Place	Date	Hour	Summary of Events and Information	Remarks and references to Appendices
	23rd		Lieut T.W. FLEWITT invalided to England.	
		4.2's	The Support Area was again shelled intermittently with 5.9's and 4.2's. Several of our 9.2's fell short, one falling on a post killing two and wounding two	
		6.45 am	One platoon of the 17th Bn SHERWOOD FORESTERS assaulted the German trenches at J.21.d. 75.30 on the MENIN ROAD. They attacked along the MENIN ROAD, one line covering by the enemy. Various Machine Gun fire was opened out on them, from the NORTH and from the SOUTH, and it was found impossible to get through the barrage to proceed with the Operation. All the party except the one officer. The whole need and Some men were found an unwoundable losses	
			4 killed 15 wounded	
	24th	5.50 am	An officer and about 30 Other Ranks were preparing down the MENIN ROAD towards the front line to make some attacks	

WAR DIARY
or
INTELLIGENCE SUMMARY.

(Erase heading not required.)

Army Form C. 2118.

Place	Date	Hour	Summary of Events and Information	Remarks and references to Appendices
	24th(?) February		Div. any interviewed to the 23rd Bn. I.H. Battalion TANK CORPS who were moved with Bren Carriers (no tanks available) and some Infantry for counter-attack in the direction of GHELUVELT. Div. was immediately ordered to take up positions of our Bns. It is reported that KIN and Bren gun posts to the South of GHELUVELT Div. were immediately relieved. Div. attacked to regain the situation and established strong K.G. posns. On seeing this the enemy opened fire with Machine Gun fire and there was no Inf. attack, but the enemy came out and ones of the party escaped the wound in man Prisoners. Our garrison suffered few casualties. Victoria Hunns, Regt. Rifles Queens were some casualties among the enemy. Casualties — 7 killed 11 wounded. 2nd Battalion were relieved by the 2nd Bn. Border Regt. and 2nd B Queen's Regt. 2nd Bn. was relieved C and D Coy the latter relieving B Coy. Relief of C and D Coy's was complete at 6.45 pm, that of B Coy only complete at 1.30 am. (25/2)	

WAR DIARY
or
INTELLIGENCE SUMMARY.
(Erase heading not required.)

Army Form C. 2118.

Place	Date	Hour	Summary of Events and Information	Remarks and references to Appendices
	25.11.		Officer i/c R. & R. Battalion endeavoured at SHRAPNEL CORNER and proceeded to LITTLE KEMMEL CAMP - Tents and Bivouacs.	
	26th		The following 17.8.05 Divisional were awarded Medals for Gallantry. Bombardier in Out during the Operations Sept 20 + 21st 1917. Bar to Military Medal:- 201452 Pte A HAWBROOK, 26285 L/Cpl G. H EATON. Military Medal:- 26-38 Pte F ADAMS, 50363 Pte A BAINES, 53106 Pte G BAXTER, 15624 Pte T BELL, 7105 Pte G BASNETT, 76168. Pte G R PARSONS, 26802 Serjt B WALKER 25438. L/Cpl A WAGGETT 69159 Pte E COOPER, 51697 Pte R COOPER, 53405 Pte G COL TOWN, Sgt H BROTHERS, 3762 Pte BIRCHLEY, 20274 Serjt A FREER, 16102, 14161 T HAYERS, 59635 Pte T WOODYARD, 30660 Serjt C GARDINER, 14186. Pte S. MELLORS, 13049 Pte PLACEY, 21/Lt TEE WILSON appointed for duty + was posted to "A" Coy	
	26.11.		The Battalion proceeded by Motor Bus to GUDZONNE FARM Camp Near CONFUSION CORNER. (N.10.d.2 & Sheet 28.)	

WAR DIARY
or
INTELLIGENCE SUMMARY.
(Erase heading not required.)

Army Form C. 2118.

Place	Date	Hour	Summary of Events and Information	Remarks and references to Appendices
	29th		Company were inspected by the Commanding Officer. Platoon football in the afternoon. Lieut T.C.O. WILLIAMS M.C. promoted Acting Captain.	
	30th		2nd Brigade General Commanding & 17 Infantry Brigade presented the Military Medal Ribbons won by M.A.O.C. Men during the Operations Sept 20th + 21st. 2nd Battalion Football XI played the 145th Field Coy R.E. & gun resulted in a win for the Battalion. Hgrts. 10-1.	
	31st		Decorations were awarded the Officers N.C.O's + men of the Battalion for Gallantry & Devotion to Duty during the Operations Sept 25th + 21st. Distinguished Service Order — Lieut Col. T.R. WEBSTER M.C. Military Cross — Lieut H. GOSLING, Lieut. A.D. PARKIN. Lieut. W.E. WRIGHT, 2Lt. G.E. WHITE 2Lt H.M. MEAKIN. 2Lt. Rev. J.F. BLOXAM. Distinguished Conduct Medal — 67096 C.S.M. ARTINSTALL W, 6328 P.S.M. COKAYNE, 29/177 Cpl. GILLATTE.	

M. Foster Lieut Col.
Commanding 16th Bn. SHERWOOD FORESTERS

—1.11.17—

War Diary 10th Royal Fus 112/39

Vol 21

WAR DIARY
or
INTELLIGENCE SUMMARY
(Erase heading not required.)

Place	Date	Hour	Summary of Events and Information	Remarks and references to Appendices
	1917		"NOVEMBER"	21A
GODAZONNE FARM	1st.		2nd Lieut J. McD. BURKE reported for duty and was posted to "C" Company. Platoon football in the afternoon.	
	2nd		The whole Battalion under the Commanding Officer proceeded to the forward area immediately South of BODMIN COPSE. The work on a new Communication Trench running from HEDGE STREET TUNNELS to the front line Companies arrived back at the Camp at 10 am (3rd).	
	3rd		Captain H.R. STEVENS M.C. returned from the 111th TRENCH MORTAR BATTERY and became acting Second in Command to the Battalion. Platoon football.	
	4th.		CHURCH PARADE was held in the Y.M.C.A. TENT near CONFUSION CORNER	

WAR DIARY
or
INTELLIGENCE SUMMARY
(Erase heading not required.)

Army Form C. 2118.

Place	Date	Hour	Summary of Events and Information	Remarks and references to Appendices
GODAZONNE FARM	4th		The Semi-finals of the Inter-Platoon football matches were Commenced. No.7 Platoon v No.14 Platoon. No.7 Platoon won by 3 goals to 1.	
	5th		Lieut. W.H.L. BULKELEY and 2nd Lieut. C.F. ROBINSON proceeded on leave to ENGLAND. Lieut. F.H. GOSSING M.O. took over temporary Command of "A" Company	
	7th		The Battalion relieved the 13th Battalion ROYAL SUSSEX REGIMENT in reserve in the POLDERHOEK SECTION and was accommodated in and around CANADA TUNNELS	
	8th		No 266714 SERGEANT J.E.CREE Battalion Signalling Sergeant awarded the MILITARY MEDAL for gallantry in rescuing a man from the Inner Support at Battalion Headquarters on October 22nd Casualties - 1 Wounded	

WAR DIARY
or
INTELLIGENCE SUMMARY.
(Erase heading not required.)

Army Form C. 2118.

Instructions regarding War Diaries and Intelligence Summaries are contained in F.S. Regs., Part II. and the Staff Manual respectively. Title pages will be prepared in manuscript.

Place	Date	Hour	Summary of Events and Information	Remarks and references to Appendices
	9th		Casualties :- Lt Wombell died.	
			Lieut A.H. STRUTT rejoined the Battalion and was posted to "B" Company.	
	10th		The Battalion relieved the 11th Battalion SHERWOOD FORESTERS in the right SUB-SECTION POLDERHOEK SECTION which to the left was on his right. 5 men were Killed and 6 wounded. Total Casualties for the day 5 Killed & 6 wounded.	
	11th		SERGEANT T.W. BARKES awarded a bar to his MILITARY MEDAL for gallantry and devotion to duty whilst on a working party by MENIN ROAD. During the day Lieut Cherry Wilkinson were very active making reconnaissances of our lines.	
	12th		The Battalion was relieved by the 1/1st HERTS REGIMENT and proceeded by Bus from SHRAPNEL CORNER to CHIPPEWA CAMP near RENINGHELST.	

WAR DIARY
or
INTELLIGENCE SUMMARY.
(Erase heading not required.)

Army Form C. 2118.

Place	Date	Hour	Summary of Events and Information	Remarks and references to Appendices
	13th		The day was devoted to cleaning up etc.	
	14th		A working party of 1 Officer and 40 other Ranks was found for the R.E.	
	15th		A further Working Party of 1 Officer and 40 other Ranks was found for the R.E.	
	16th		2nd Lieut. G.F. WHITE M.C. proceeded on leave to ENGLAND. The Battalion continued at CHIPPEWA CAMP and provided 4 SHRAPNEL CORNER, HOOGE to BODMIN COPSE relieving the 1/1st HERTS REGIMENT in SUPPORT to the POLDERHOEK SECTION. Two Companies were in BODMIN COPSE one at the TOWER and one east of VELDHOEK. During the night the Enemy sent over a number of Gas Shells into BODMIN COPSE and around the TOWER but the result was 24 men were found slightly affected but was quite well as nothing could be detected at the time and the men were only afflicted within hours after.	

CAPTAIN P.L.E. EADIE took over the duties of MEDICAL OFFICER in charge of the Battalion

WAR DIARY
or
INTELLIGENCE SUMMARY.

(Erase heading not required.)

Army Form C. 2118.

Place	Date	Hour	Summary of Events and Information	Remarks and references to Appendices
	16.		VICE CAPTAIN S.J.L. LINDEMAN SICK.	
	17.		Lieut Col J.R. WEBSTER DSO, MC. proceeded on leave to PARIS and CAPTAIN H.R. STEVENS MC assumed temporary Command of the Battalion. The Battalion furnished working parties for the R.Es and Carrying parties for the Brigade. 2 KILLED, 4 WOUNDED.	
	18.		The Battalion relieved the 17th BATTALION SHERWOOD FORESTERS on the right of Battalion front POTDERHOEK SECTION.	
	19.		The day was fairly quiet - intermittent Shelling along the MENIN ROAD and vicinity. The Support was active from direction of LEWIS HOUSE. Machine Guns were very active at night - traversing the front line and all approaches to the front line. 2 KILLED	

WAR DIARY
or
INTELLIGENCE SUMMARY.
(Erase heading not required.)

Army Form C. 2118.

Place	Date	Hour	Summary of Events and Information	Remarks and references to Appendices
	20th		A Shell entered our M.D. "Company" dug outs Killing our asst. and our adj Lieut 2nd Lieut T. McD. BURKE was wounded by a sniper. Casualties - 3 KILLED 4 WOUNDED The Battalion was relieved by the 16th CHESHIRE REGIMENT and entrained at the HALT - near ZILLEBEKE - proceeding to RIDGE WOOD CAMP. Relief was complete by 7.30 p.m.	
	21st		The day was devoted to cleaning up etc. CAPTAIN GOMPERZ RAMC took over the MEDICAL CHARGE of the Battalion vice CAPTAIN PIKE SICK	
	22nd		LIEUT. COL. T. R. WEBSTER DSO, MC, returning from leave at PARIS, took over Command of the 119th Brigade vice Brigadier General G. ARMYTAGE DSO on leave in ENGLAND.	

WAR DIARY
or
INTELLIGENCE SUMMARY.

(Erase heading not required.)

Army Form C. 2118.

Place	Date	Hour	Summary of Events and Information	Remarks and references to Appendices
	24th		The Battalion travelled from RIDGE WOOD to OUDERDOM STATION from where it travelled to ABEELE. From ABEELE the Battalion travelled to billets in the vicinity of L.13 Central (MAP SHEET 24) - about 1½ miles N of ABEELE	
	25th		Church Parade was held at 2 Coy Left Billet. Lieut Col J.R.WEBSTER DSO MC returned from the 117th Infantry Brigade and resumed Command of the Battalion. Major R.W.ILLINGWORTH M.C., The Rev. T.E.BUXHAM, M.C. and Lieut R.C.DAVIES M.C. proceeded on leave to ENGLAND. Lieut F.H.GOSLING M.C. proceeded to ENGLAND to attend a G.H.Q.s Signalling Course at DUNSTABLE. The following officers joined the Battalion for duty:- Lieut M. DRYNAN, 2nd Lieut C.A.G.MOORE, 2nd Lieut W.C.WHITWORTH, 2nd Lieut E.V.SMALLEY, and 2nd Lieut A.G.HOLLOWAY	
	26th		Training was carried out in the vicinity of Billets	

WAR DIARY
or
INTELLIGENCE SUMMARY.
(Erase heading not required.)

Army Form C. 2118.

Place	Date	Hour	Summary of Events and Information	Remarks and references to Appendices
	27th		The Battalion Carried out training in vicinity of Billets	M
	28th		Corporal E.A.EGERTON awarded the VICTORIA CROSS	W
	29th		The Battalion Bivouacked by march route to GODSWERVELDE and from thence by motor lorries to LA BRIQUE.	
			2nd Lieut. H.M. HARRISON proceeded on leave to ENGLAND	
	30th		Taking over new Outpost to the C.R.E. VIII Corps for revisit as reconnaissance patrols from the Armee area	N
			Lieut. I.A. GOTTHARD invalided to ENGLAND (18/11/17)	W

A.R.Moon Lt Colonel
Commanding 16th Battalion Sherwood Foresters

WAR DIARY
or
INTELLIGENCE SUMMARY.
(Erase heading not required.)

Army Form C. 2118.

16 North'n R'lly

16/22

Place	Date	Hour	Summary of Events and Information	Remarks and references to Appendices
	1917		December	
ST JEAN	1st		Lieut Col. J.R. WEBSTER D.S.O. M.C. Proceeded on leave to England. Captain A.R. STEVENS M.C. assuming temporary Command of the Battalion	
	2nd		Captain A.R. STEVENS M.C. ceased 2nd in Command of the Battalion. 2nd Lieut G.F. WHITE M.C. returned from leave in England	
	3rd		2nd Lieut. H.M. MEAKIN M.C. proceeded on a course at the X'th Corps School	
	6th		From November 30 - until this date nothing notable happened. Battalion were found for the C.R.E. VIII # Corps.	
	7th		The Battalion proceeded by train to ABEELE and took up Billets in the STEENVOORDE Area	22A
ABEELE	8th		2nd Lieut. F.G. STEWARD joined for duty	Tally

WAR DIARY
or
INTELLIGENCE SUMMARY.
(Erase heading not required.)

Army Form C. 2118.

Place	Date	Hour	Summary of Events and Information	Remarks and references to Appendices
ABEELE	8th		Lieut. A.D. PARKIN M.C. rejoined	
	9th		The Battalion entrained at ABEELE and proceeded to LOTTINGHEN thence by	
			route March to Billets at QUESQUES and VERVAH	
			A + B Companies at Headquarters at QUESQUE and C+D Companies at VERVAH	
			2nd Lieut. J.B. BUSWELL proceeded on a Musketry Course at N.W. School	
QUESQUES &	10th		2nd Lieut. T POWELL asked for duty	
VERVAH	12th		2nd Lieuts. R.N. BARKER, C.E. ALLEN and W.H. FOXON reported for duty	
	13th		Lieut. R.C. DAVIES M.C. rejoined from leave	
	14th		Battalion Cookery and Bluster thereof was Carried out on the ground plan	
	15th		The Rev. J.F. BIGHAM M.C. brought back the instruments to form a Brass Band	
	18th			

WAR DIARY
or
INTELLIGENCE SUMMARY.

(Erase heading not required.)

Army Form C. 2118.

Place	Date	Hour	Summary of Events and Information	Remarks and references to Appendices
QUESQUES	19th		Lieut Col. T.R. WEBSTER DSO MC returned from leave in England	
VERVAL			"D" Company also the Battalion left for Cambelhurst in the Divisional Cross Country Run	
	20th		The Battalion was inspected by the G.O.C. 39th Division who congratulated such officers N.C.O and men who had been awarded a ribbon for gallantry during (Once the operations of September 20th 1917)	
	21st		"D" Company won the Brigade Heat for the Competition in the Divisional Cross Country Run by four (4) points	
	22nd		"B" Company Football XI. Played Company of the 16th Battalion Rifle BRIGADE on our ground	
			"B" Company won 3 goals to 1	

WAR DIARY
or
INTELLIGENCE SUMMARY.
(Erase heading not required.)

Army Form C. 2118.

Place	Date	Hour	Summary of Events and Information	Remarks and references to Appendices
QUESQUES & VERVAH	23rd		The Brigade Tent for the Divisional TUG-OF-WAR were pulled off and our Sergeants Combined Team was beaten by "B" Battery of the 7th Battalion Sherwood Foresters who also went to the Bull Ring (the winner were the 12th Battalion Rifle Brigade. The Band made its first public appearance and played for half an hour round the village.	
	24th		Lieut. A.H. STRUTT and 2nd Lieut. B.T. McPHERSON returned from Courses. Each Company held a Smoker in their respective Billets in the various Corporals and men of the Companys Messes. Special food was provided and P.R.I funds also Beer and Cigarettes. About midnight the Band played Carols to the various Messes in the Village	
	25th	6.0 pm	At 6.0 pm the Senior N.C.O's and Warrant Officers held their Xmas Dinner in the Village School.	

WAR DIARY
or
INTELLIGENCE SUMMARY.

Army Form C. 2118.

Place	Date	Hour	Summary of Events and Information	Remarks and references to Appendices
QUESNES & VERNAH	25th	11.30 am	A Service XMAS Guard was held in the Battalion Headquarters Mess for all the Officers of the Battalion. A Kind Piano had greatly to the enjoyment of the Xmas festivities.	
	27th	10.30 am	At 10.30 am the final of the Divisional Inter-Brigade Cross Country Runs. The 118th Brigade was represented by the 118th Machine Gun Company. The 117th Brigade by "B" Company of the 16th Battn. SHERWOOD FORESTERS. The 116th Brigade by a Company of the 14th Battn. HAMPSHIRE REGIMENT. Runners over a Number of fences both hurdles and brooks. The team scoring the lowest Number of points being the Winners. The 117th Brigade ("B" Coy. 16th SHERWOOD FORESTERS) Won & the team were the first in at a score of 205 points. The 116th Brigade Came second with a score of 389 points. The 118th Brigade was third with a score of 556 points. At the mess the Divisional Commander presented a silver cup to the Winning Team. A silver Medal to each of the members of the Winning Team.	

Army Form C. 2118.

WAR DIARY
or
INTELLIGENCE SUMMARY.
(Erase heading not required.)

Instructions regarding War Diaries and Intelligence Summaries are contained in F. S. Regs., Part II. and the Staff Manual respectively. Title pages will be prepared in manuscript.

Place	Date	Hour	Summary of Events and Information	Remarks and references to Appendices
QUESQUES & VERVAN	27th		Below is a nominal roll of the Wounded Officers.	
			2nd Lieut. A.B. STEVENS M.C. 2nd Lieut. G.E. WHITE M.C. 2nd Lieut. G.A.G. MOORE.	
			2nd Lieut. R.N. BARKER. 2nd Lieut. A.G. HOLLOWAY No.26431 Sergeant WILSON F.A.	
			No.18491 Sergeant SARGESON J. No.70161 Corporal ROBINSON E.	
			No.32516 L/Corporal FENTON H. No.26893 L/Corporal WOOD W.C.	
			No.18144 L/Corporal REST H. No.16458 L/Corporal ADAMS F. No.R/1963 Private	
			DUNCAN C. No.28189 Private WALKER J. No.212367 Private BOTTROFF R.W.	
			No.27412 Private HAWKINS W. No.40124 Private BEST J. No.98035 Private	
			RANDALL T. No.76119 Private BOYNE A. No.51340 Private BRAKE W.M.	
			Lieut. Col. J.L. WEBSTER D.S.O. M.C. admitted to Field Ambulance sick	
	28th		The Battalion moved by route march from QUESQUES and VERVAN Billets to	
			SENINGHEM. The Battalion Lewis guns were conveyed to same by the Lorried Column.	
SENINGHEM	29th		The Battalion proceeded by route march from SENINGHEM to WIZERNES thence by train to	
			ST. JEAN STATION and was accommodated in huts and tents at IRISH FARM.	

Army Form C. 2118.

WAR DIARY
or
INTELLIGENCE SUMMARY.
(Erase heading not required.)

Instructions regarding War Diaries and Intelligence Summaries are contained in F. S. Regs., Part II. and the Staff Manual respectively. Title pages will be prepared in manuscript.

Place	Date	Hour	Summary of Events and Information	Remarks and references to Appendices
ALBERTA	30th		The Battalion relieved the 2nd Battalion MANCHESTER REGIMENT becoming Battalion in SUPPORT in the ALBERTA SECTION and accommodated in Dug Outs on the valley of the STEEN BEEK	(1)
	31st		The S.O.S. was sent up from the LIGHT FRONT Battalion at 2.30 am. The Battalion "STOOD TO" but was not required in consequence. 2nd Lieut. B.T. McPHERSON was admitted to visit reconnaissance area.	(2)

A.R. Nixon, Major
Commanding 10. Battalion Alberta Foresters

A6945 Wt. W14422/M1160 350,000 12/16 D. D. & L. Forms/C./2118/14.

WAR DIARY or INTELLIGENCE SUMMARY

10th Sherwood Foresters

Army Form C. 2118.

23A

Place	Date	Hour	Summary of Events and Information	Remarks and references to Appendices
			January 1918	
STEENBEEK	1st		For his work as Sherwood Foresters (Notts & Derby) during the whole of 1917 Lt Col (A/Brigadier) Genl G.A. ARMYTAGE D.S.O. Commanding 85th Inf Bde 28th Div of French Armies was awarded the C.M.G.	
			Lieut Col G. Heath Stepney D.S.O. was awarded a bar to his D.S.O.	
			Lt. Col A.W. VINYARD D.S.O. late London Fusiliers of this Battalion was awarded a bar to his D.S.O.	
			Sergt ? Quartermaster Sergt BRYANT was awarded the Military Cross	
	2nd			
	3rd		The Battn returned to the Battle. STEENBEEK forestation to the S.A.L	
			Average strength	
			Offrs 31 Other Ranks 3. Bombardiers & Mentioned in Dispatches	
	4th		Casualties. 1 Wounded	

Army Form C. 2118.

WAR DIARY
or
INTELLIGENCE SUMMARY
(Erase heading not required.)

Place	Date	Hour	Summary of Events and Information	Remarks and references to Appendices
STEENBECK	5th		Casualties 2 killed 3 wounded	app
	6th		Casualties 1 wounded	app
	7th		The Battalion was relieved by 1st Aus Black Watch Regiment and marched to DAMBRE CAMP	app
DAMBRE CAMP	8th		Rest. New Draft Offs 1	
	9th		Cleaning and refitting	app
	10th		Captain J. C. Williams MC Lieut C. F. Garland and Lieut S.V.B. Wass proceeded on leave to ENGLAND	app
	11th		Captain S.H. Lindsay proceeded on leave to ENGLAND	app

WAR DIARY
or
INTELLIGENCE SUMMARY.
(Erase heading not required.)

Army Form C. 2118.

Place	Date	Hour	Summary of Events and Information	Remarks and references to Appendices
DRABBLE (CWP)	11th		"B" Coy left 16th Batt. entrained Eastern Ont. D. Coy of 15th Batt.	A.192
			Kings Own Rifle Corps. 5 guns & 11th-A of the Durham Kershire Brigade.	
	12th		The Battalion proceeded on March of Entries into the Firm line.	A.193
	13th		Capt. P. F. BURROWS M.C. returned from Battalion Fire Hospital.	A.193
			2nd Lieut. H. DRABBLE joined the Unit.	
			Capt. P. F. BURROWS M.C. proceeded on leave to ENGLAND.	
	14		Lieutenant Ewin's received from the NOTTINGHAMSHIRE Cheshire Brits	A.194
			Command posted distributed to the Coys.	
CANAL BANK	15th		The Battalion moved to the Dug Outs on the CANAL BANK.	A.194
			The Coy are now much scattered up the banks of the CANAL	
			holding parties and of suchs and supplies each day to help for Comp C.O. and
			WINCHESTER Dug Outs

Army Form C. 2118.

WAR DIARY
or
INTELLIGENCE SUMMARY.
(Erase heading not required.)

Instructions regarding War Diaries and Intelligence Summaries are contained in F. S. Regs., Part II. and the Staff Manual respectively. Title pages will be prepared in manuscript.

Place	Date	Hour	Summary of Events and Information	Remarks and references to Appendices
CANAL BANK	15th		Captn. L.T.B. Harwood returned from leave	C.X.P
	16th		Revd. Paulin was found	C.X.P
	17th		Lieut. Gardner - Webster. D.S.O. M.O. Marked A. for duty	C.X.P
			Revd. Paulin sent south	
	18th		2nd Lieuts. L.O. Smith, N.S. Dye. F. Nurse. G.E. Wood reported for duty	C.X.P
			and W. Okey Smith rejoined from leave - arrived	
	19th		2nd Lieut. B.T. McPherson evacuated to England 14-1-18	C.X.P
			2nd Lieut. T.M. Donald Burke evacuated to England 11-1-18	
	21st		2nd Lieut. H.B. Buswell proceeded on Charge of drawing party to assist R.E. Co. from New Area	C.X.P

WAR DIARY
or
INTELLIGENCE SUMMARY.
(Erase heading not required.)

Army Form C. 2118.

Instructions regarding War Diaries and Intelligence Summaries are contained in F. S. Regs., Part II. and the Staff Manual respectively. Title pages will be prepared in manuscript.

Place	Date	Hour	Summary of Events and Information	Remarks and references to Appendices
ROAD CAMP	11th		1st Battalion moved to ROAD CAMP near WATOU	
			Lieutn. S.F. ETCHEY "A" Coy reported to Battalion from Hospital	
	12th		2nd Lieut. K. L'ESTRANGE reported to duty	
				C of E
	13th		1st Battalion relieved 15th Battn Yorkshire SHERWOOD FORESTERS at Poperin	
			Relief - 16th Battn. Sherwood Foresters to 9 p.m. - 1st Battalion Sherwood Foresters 9 p.m.	6 C of E
			"Town"	
			Sgt. SHERROCK E. "B"	
			Sgt. WATSON J. "B" Water Hastings M.O.	
			Pte BAINES F. "AHQ" Sgt. WALKER B "O" 2nd Lieut. TOWELL	
			Sgt. SMART E. "B" 1st Pte SHEPPARD Q.M. 3 Coal CAVILL T. 2nd CORHAMPTON A.S.C. W. RIDOUT R.E.	

War Diary & Intelligence Summary.

Place	Date	
SUZANNE	24th	The Battalion left ROAD CAMP and proceeded by train from PROVEN Station by night to MERICOURT L'ABBÉ, detraining at 9.30 am on the 25th and those of March route to SUZANNE when Billets were taken over.
	25th	Brigadier Gen. G.A. ARMYTAGE. C.M.G. D.S.O. inspected the Battalion on the line of march and expressed his satisfaction with the smartness, turnout and general discipline of the Battalion. The Battalion transferred to XIIIth Corps VIth Army. The Bands used their instruments for the first time on the line of march and were congratulated by the Commanding Officers on the label Colours made.
	26th	The Battalion's estate and Command of Trench Army huts and entrenched lorries were found to be in need of repairs Considerable improvements were made by each Beserers.

WAR DIARY
or
INTELLIGENCE SUMMARY.
(Erase heading not required.)

Army Form C. 2118.

Instructions regarding War Diaries and Intelligence
Summaries are contained in F. S. Regs., Part II.
and the Staff Manual respectively. Title pages
will be prepared in manuscript.

Place	Date	Hour	Summary of Events and Information	Remarks and references to Appendices
SUZANNE	2/2		Divine Service was held	App
			The Commanding Officer and Orderly Officers reconnoitred the approaches to ST QUENTIN.	
	29th		The Battalion proceeded by Route March from CARNOY to PERONNE thence by March Route to MOISLAINS where they remained over night.	App
			11th Infant Brigade relieved this Battn infant Supports for the night from 30/31st and 31st/1st February.	
			At 10 A.M. 68th Boxing Contest took place WATOU on several 2nd Lt No. 5105 Ernest HARRISON. T. Company Wells Wright now left to Captain Army Chamberlain	
	30th	1.30 pm	QUARTERMASTER A/Lieut H.C. Traslaved to to 14th Convalescent Camp	App
			as Quarter-Master and Assistant Adjutant	
			2nd Lieut T. POWELL assumed the duties of Quartermaster.	

Army Form C. 2118.

WAR DIARY
or
INTELLIGENCE SUMMARY.
(Erase heading not required.)

Place	Date	Hour	Summary of Events and Information	Remarks and references to Appendices
RAILWAY CAMP	30th		The Battalion moved by March Route and Rail to RAILWAY CAMP	
HEUDECOURT			HEUDECOURT, being met by Billeting Officer the 24th Battalion NORTHUMBERLAND FUSILIERS.	
			On the night of the 30/31 31st the Camp was bombed by Hostile Aircraft. Casualties 1 Killed 5 Wounded	
	31st		The Battalion watched with interest Protection of Kite Balloon against attacks by Hostile aircraft. C.O. and Padre.	
			Captain S.M. LINDEMAN Captain T.O. WILLIAMS M.C. Captain J.F. BURROWS M.C. Lieut. C.F. GARLAND and 2nd Lieut. B.G.B. WYLES returned from leave to ENGLAND.	

R. Moir
Commanding 6th Battalion Northumberland Fusiliers

Army Form C. 2118.

WAR DIARY
or
INTELLIGENCE SUMMARY.
(Erase heading not required.)

1/1th Sherwood Foresters

Place	Date	Hour	Summary of Events and Information	Remarks and references to Appendices
HEUDECOURT			"February" 1918	
	3rd		The Battalion relieved the 1/7th Battalion SHERWOOD FORESTERS in the VAUCELETTE FARM Sector - GOUZEAUCOURT RIGHT Sector. Right sub Sector.	
			a most difficult & dangerous relief - which continued until 4pm 4th Sergt. Therefore to able to shewed to confer 200 yards [...] had two by day on night, and yet we [...] to give the men hot meals at any time	
			The Trenches are extraordinarily good and with a little work can be made as good as the Enemy Canal-one The retirement on them.	B
	4th		Major H.K. STEVENS MC proceeded on a Months leave in ENGLAND	
			2/Lieut. H.B. BUSHELL proceeded on Leave to ENGLAND.	Ba
	5th		Lt./Adjt. H.M. HARRISON proceeded to ENGLAND for 6 months tour of duty at home.	Bb
			An Inter-Company relief took place	
	7th		"B" and "D" Companies relieving "C" and "A" Companies respectively in the front line.	
			2nd Lieut. A.M. NEAGIN MC proceeded to ENGLAND for 6 months duty at home.	Bc
	8th		Under the not solving N Army act the Battalions in a Brigade had to be chosen which extent to the Reports Started to knock out. It seems such discussed that the 1/7th Battalion SHERWOOD FORESTERS should be disbanded. Numerically the Battalion was the Strongest, it was eventually decided that the	

24A

WAR DIARY
or
INTELLIGENCE SUMMARY.
(Erase heading not required.)

Army Form C. 2118.

Place	Date	Hour	Summary of Events and Information	Remarks and references to Appendices
HEUDECOURT	8th		11th Battalion SHERWOOD FORESTERS ceased to be disbanded in effect. The disbandment took place on the 8th February. Its officers N.C.O's and men being posted to other Battalions of the Regiment. The undermentioned were posted to the 16th Battalion:	
			Captain A. KERR. attached Divisional Headquarters	
			Lieut. J.W.T. MILLAR DSO Doy posted to A Company 16th SHERWOOD FORESTERS	
			,, M.A. FAWSSEN MC ,, B ,, ,, ,,	
			,, G. REECE attached Brigade Headquarters	
			,, N. DEXTER MC posted to A Company ,, ,,	
			2nd Lieut. W.E. BOSWELL ,, A ,, ,, ,,	
			,, C.H. ROLLASON ,, A ,, ,, ,,	
			,, G. POWELL ,, A ,, ,, ,,	
			,, L. SURRIDGE ,, A ,, ,, ,,	
			and 100 other Ranks (150 to) A ,, 50 to B, C & D Coys of the	
			16. SHERWOOD FORESTERS	
			The remaining Officers deemed to disband the recent "A" Company and to form a nucleus, with the Officers and 150 other Ranks joined the 17th Battalion SHERWOOD FORESTERS as staff, absorbed filling up the remaining Companies with the Officers and other ranks to form its own A Coy. A short list also of Disbanded Battn during Decembr and recently where as of whom afterwards died of Wounds	98

WAR DIARY
or
INTELLIGENCE SUMMARY

Army Form C. 2118.

Place	Date	Hour	Summary of Events and Information	Remarks and references to Appendices
HEUDECOURT	9th		Six Officers NCOs known from the 17th Battalion SHERWOOD FORESTERS joined the Battalion and were posted as stated above.	
	11th		Captain D.W. STEVENS. M.C. proceeded on leave to ENGLAND. 2 men wounded. A Draft of 5 other ranks joined the Battalion.	
	12th		57016. C.S.M. ARKINSTALL DCM. proceeded to join the 1st Battalion H.A.C. at G.H.Q. leaving instructions to ENGLAND to take up a Command Commission.	
			The Battalion was relieved by the 11th Battalion KINGS ROYAL RIFLE CORPS and proceeded to RAILWAY CAMP HEUDECOURT, 1½ miles behind the front line where it was accommodated in huts. The Trenches left had been Constantly unproved during the last month every being Extended in time.	
	13th		The day was devoted to rest and Cleaning up. Captain W.E WRIGHT M.C proceeded on leave to ENGLAND. Working Parties were found for the 178th Tunnelling Coy and 227th Field Coy R.E.	
	14th		LEUT A.D PARKIN M.C. proceeded to ENGLAND for 8 Months tour of duty at home.	

WAR DIARY or INTELLIGENCE SUMMARY

Army Form C. 2118.

Place	Date	Hour	Summary of Events and Information	Remarks and references to Appendices
HEBUTERNE	15.12		The Battalion Football XI played the 13th Battalion GLOSTER team, winning by 6 goals - Nil	
	16.12		The Battalion relieved the 16th Battalion RIFLE BRIGADE in the GOUZEAUCOURT RIGHT SECTOR. Left S.F (Dexter). During the night the Enemy aircraft was very active on back areas obtaining direct hits on Horse Lines. 10 Reinforcements arrived	
	17.12		Captain J.W.J. NIHHAR DSO DCM Proceeded on leave to ENGLAND	
	18.12 to 20.12		The enemy shelled our own front line from VAUQUELETTE FARM SECTOR. Fought for supplies. Marked Gun Activity at nights. No Enemy Shelled the garrisons but very little. Then much work was needed forming Saps etc., laying duckboards and making general improvements. Three Companies were in the front line and one in support, and were directed to have no working parties during its 8 days tour.	
	21.12		At H.Q. and the Enemy bombarded the Rotations on our right S.O.S was sent up and the Battalion Stood to Arms but no further raid on attack was developed. 2nd Lieut. SURRIDGE proceeded on leave to ENGLAND.	

Place	Date	Hour	Summary of Events and Information	Remarks and references to Appendices
ECOIVRT	22nd		Casualties - 2O.R's wounded by M. Arbred (Gun Fire) 2 O.R's accidentally wounded	Y
	24th		Lieut N.F. DEXTER M.C. was accidentally and seriously wounded by loading of fuse trigger in which and falling on a rifle with fixed bayonet. The 17th Battalion KINGS ROYAL RIFLE CORPS relieved the 6th Battalion RIFLE BRIGADE in our right subsector and the RIFLE BRIGADE relieved this Battalion. Relief was completed by 9.15 pm. on which day the Battalion proceeded. "A" and "C" Companies each Battalion Headquarters B and D Companies to the RAILWAY Embankment to RAILWAY CAMP HEQUECOURT (Ref S73)	Y
	25th		The day was spent resting, cleaning up and eating	Y
	26th		Captain D.W. STEVENS M.C. assumed temporary command of "B" Company and Lieut R.C. DAVIES M.C. temporary command of "D" Company	Y
	26th		Captain P.E. BURROWS M.C. and Lieut G.F. WHITE M.C. proceeded to ENGLAND to transfer to the INDIAN ARMY Lieut A.H. STRUTT and 2nd/Lieut E.E. WILSON proceeded on leave to ENGLAND	Y

WAR DIARY
or
INTELLIGENCE SUMMARY

Army Form C. 2118.

Place	Date	Hour	Summary of Events and Information	Remarks and references to Appendices
HODECOURT	26th		The Battalion found Working Parties for the 204th Field Coy. R.E. and 13th GLOSTER (PIONEER BATTALION)	
	27th		Working Parties were found from 204th Field Coy. R.E. Weather unsettled which interfered with the afternoon.	
	28th		The battalion was relieved by the 13th Gloucestershire Regiment and after being relieved the 1/6th CHESHIRE REGIMENT and Brigade moved to Camp.	

R. Webster Lieut Col
Commanding 1/6th Battalion Cheshire Regiment

117th Inf.Bde.
39th Div.

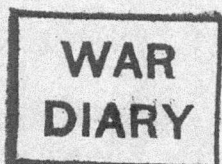

16th BATTN. THE SHERWOOD FORESTERS (NOTTINGHAMSHIRE AND DERBYSHIRE REGIMENT).

M A R C H

1 9 1 8

16th Sherwood Foresters

Army Form C. 2118.

06125

WAR DIARY
or
INTELLIGENCE SUMMARY.
(Erase heading not required.)

Place	Date	Hour	Summary of Events and Information	Remarks and references to Appendices
	1918		"March"	
DESSART WOOD CAMP	1st		Working Parties were found for 29th Field Coy R.E. Captain P.E. BURROWS MC. and Lieut. G.F. WHITE MC. struck off the strength of the Battalion being transferred to the Indian Army	
	3rd		The Commanding Officer inspected all reinforcements which had arrived since February 13th During Second who held Working Parties were found for Work on YELLOW SYSTEM in front of QUEENS CROSS.	
	4th		Draft of 41 other ranks arrived	
	5th		"B" Company's Football team played a team chosen from the remainder of the Battalion. Result "B" Company 1 goal. Remainder of the Battalion nil Draft of 44 O.R's arrived. Captain T.W.J. MILLAR D.S.O. D.C.M. Returned from leave in England Working parties were found as usual	

WAR DIARY
or
INTELLIGENCE SUMMARY.
(Erase heading not required.)

Army Form C. 2118.

Place	Date	Hour	Summary of Events and Information	Remarks and references to Appendices
DESSART WOOD CAMP	6th		A Football Match was played between the 16th Battalion SHERWOOD FORESTERS and the 5th CAMERON HIGHLANDERS. Result :- 16th Battalion SHERWOOD FORESTERS 1 Goal 5th CAMERON HIGHLANDERS Nil. Working Parties were found as usual	A.S.B.
	7th		Working Parties were found as usual. In addition to working on the YELLOW SYSTEM the Battalion was also engaged in burying Cable backward from this SYSTEM.	A.S.B.
	8th		The Semi-Final Us. Company Divisional Cup was played between "B" Company 16th Battalion SHERWOOD FORESTERS and "B" Company 4/5th BLACK WATCH Result :- "B" Company 16th SHERWOOD FORESTERS 1 Goal 4/5th BLACK WATCH Nil. A Company on the Rifle Range. Working parties were found for the 234th Field Company R.E.	A.S.B.
	9th		2nd Lieut. L. SURRIDGE rejoined the Battalion from leave in England Summer Leave Came into force.	A.S.B.

WAR DIARY
or
INTELLIGENCE SUMMARY.
(Erase heading not required.)

Army Form C. 2118.

Place	Date	Hour	Summary of Events and Information	Remarks and references to Appendices
DESSART WOOD CAMP	10th		Divine Service was held.	
			A Return Football Match was played between 16th Battalion SHERWOOD FORESTERS and 5th CAMERON HIGHLANDERS. Result - 16th Battalion SHERWOOD FORESTERS 1 goal 5th CAMERON HIGHLANDERS Nil.	
			Working Parties were found as usual.	166
	11th		Boxing and Tug O' War Practices were held. Working Parties were found as usual. Parties relieved the Battalion from the 119th Brigade Pioneers Company and the 227th Field Company R.E.s	
	12th		Working Parties were found as usual. Range firing. Two men wounded and at duty. Company football in the afternoon. Captain W.E. WRIGHT M.C. & 2nd Lieut. W.E. BOSWELL proceeded to LA TOUQUET on a Lewis Gun Course.	163

WAR DIARY
or
INTELLIGENCE SUMMARY.

(Erase heading not required.)

Army Form C. 2118.

Place	Date	Hour	Summary of Events and Information	Remarks and references to Appendices
DESSART WOOD CAMP.	13th		Working Parties were found as usual, Range firing by Companies	
			2nd Lieut. F.T. STEWARD proceeded to England for transfer to the Machine Gun Corps	
	14th		A/Lieut. Col. J.R. WEBSTER DSO MC. Promoted TEMPORARY LIEUT. Col. as from 15/11/17	
	15th		Captain & Adjutant S. FLINNEY M.C. Struck of the Strength of the Battalion	
	17th		Working Parties were found as usual, Church Parade.	
			Lieut A.H. STRUTT & 2nd Lieut. E.E. WILSON rejoined the Battalion from leave in England	
	18th		The following to the result of the Inter Coys Company Shooting Competition	
			1st "C" Company	
			2nd Headquarters Company	
			3rd "A" Company	
			4th "D" "	
			5th "B" Company	

WAR DIARY
or
INTELLIGENCE SUMMARY.
(Erase heading not required.)

Army Form C. 2118.

Place	Date	Hour	Summary of Events and Information	Remarks and references to Appendices
DESSART WOOD CAMP	18th		"C" Company beat Headquarters Company after shooting off a tie	
			The following were the best scores:-	
			Sergeant JEAVONS W. "C" Coy. 80.	
			Private DALE C.N. "D" 78	
			" SILVESTON J. "H.Q." 78	
			Lieut. R.M. DRYNAN "A" 72	
			C.S.M. COKAYNE A. DCM. "C" 70	
			Lieut. Col. J.R. WEBSTER D.S.O. M.C. 67	
			C.S.M. BULLIMORE R. DCM "D" Coy 67	
			Private HUNT R. "H.Q." 66	
			R.S.M. PEPPER T. M.C. "H.Q." Coy 64	
			R.Q.M.S. BRINDLEY T. " 63	
			Private CAIN L. "B" 60.	
			Lance Corpl. RADBURN G. "A" 59	
			Private SMITH W. "B" 58.	
			" WINDER A. "B" 57	
			Sergeant TRANTER E. "A" 56	
			MAJOR H.R. STEVENS. M.O. "H.Q." 55.	
			The Best eight of the Battalion are as follows:-	
			"A" Company 1 "C" Company 2	
			"B" " 2 "D" " 2	
			Headquarters Company 3	
	19th		Working Parties were found as usual. Companies on Range firing.	

Army Form C. 2118.

WAR DIARY
or
INTELLIGENCE SUMMARY.
(Erase heading not required.)

Instructions regarding War Diaries and Intelligence Summaries are contained in F.S. Regs., Part II. and the Staff Manual respectively. Title pages will be prepared in manuscript.

Place	Date	Hour	Summary of Events and Information	Remarks and references to Appendices
DESSART WOOD CAMP.	20th		Captain D.W. STEVENS M.C. proceeded to England for 6 Months tour of duty	W.B
SOREL LE GRAND.	21st		Heavy Hostile Shelling and Gas Bombardment Commenced at 11.30 and a few Shells dropping on the Camp. The Battalion left the Camp at 1am and travelled to SOREL WOOD in Close fig and Heavy Gas "Box Barrage" being active. 23 Pros. Casualties about 8 am MATOR H.P. STEVENS M.C. and Captain J.W.J. MILLAR DSO DCM and 110 Details moved to HAUT ALLAINES at 9 pm orders were received for the Battalion to proceed and dig a central line at LONGUEVAL. On Completion the line was garrisoned.	
LONGUEVAL.	22nd		During the morning along the Battle front Hostile began to fall back and by 2.30 am the Battalion was in touch with the Enemy. Heavy Machine Gun fire from Enemy Aircraft. Battalions on the Flanks were attacked at 3 am and at 6.30 am Tanks having Caused way the Battalion had Orders to work around by Matross to BOIS DE BEURRE through Violent heavy fought by A & C Companies Assembly was Completed at BOIS DE BEURRE at 8 am at 11 am the Battalion moved into Support of the 17th Battalion K.R.R. Corps and 16th Battalion RIFLE BRIGADE who were holding the GREEN LINE at TINCOURT WOOD.	W.B

WAR DIARY or INTELLIGENCE SUMMARY.

Army Form C. 2118.

(Erase heading not required.)

Place	Date	Hour	Summary of Events and Information	Remarks and references to Appendices
	22nd		Captain L.T.B. HARRISON took Command of the Battalion vice LIEUT. COL. T.R. WEBSTER D.S.O. M.C. who was wounded and believed taken prisoner.	
MONT. ST. QUENTIN.	23rd		At 8 a.m. Orders were received to withdraw and take up a new front BEUNE to NURLU-PERONNE ROAD. At 1 p.m. the Battalion withdrew from this line under pressure and took up a new position at MONT ST QUENTIN. MAJOR H.R. STEVENS. M.C. returned from DETAILS and assumed Command of the Battalion. The Battalion was nearly surrounded during the fighting at this front and fell back fighting towards CLERY. Here the Battalion was re-organised and formed a defensive flank along with small parties of various Units. An enemy attack was repulsed.	
CLERY.	24th		During the day the line was withdrawn across the river and at 8 p.m. the Bridge was blown up.	
HERBECOURT.	25th		A Quiet day. At 11 p.m. the Enemy attacked heavily on flanks and the Battalion was nearly surrounded and withdrew to a line near HERBECOURT and dug in.	
	26th		The Enemy heavily attacked our line again, capturing HERBECOURT and another withdrawal was necessary.	

WAR DIARY
or
INTELLIGENCE SUMMARY.

(Erase heading not required.)

Army Form C. 2118.

Place	Date	Hour	Summary of Events and Information	Remarks and references to Appendices
PROYART.	26th		The Battalion fell back fighting all the way forming rearguard action to the Division and forced the main line at PROYART. The Battalion was heavily shelled.	Appx A.B
MORCOURT	27th		The Enemy delivered heavy infantry attacks at daybreak. Enormous casualties were inflicted by our Rifle and Lewis Gun fire throughout the day. The Division on our right having given way the Battalion withdrew to high ground at MORCOURT fighting stubbornly.	A.B 95
CAYEUX	28th		Information was received about 1 am that the Enemy had crossed the SOMME further south and had taken LAMOTTE in our rear and was still attacking the Battalion who retired to CAYEUX by sections and took up a position in a wood. The Enemy attacked and was repulsed with heavy losses. the prisoners being left in our hands. Owing to the units adjacent to the Enemy in our rear the Battalion was forced to withdraw to high ground near AUBERCOURT Enemy shelling still being very heavy.	A.B.C
AUBERCOURT	29th		The Enemy put down a heavy barrage on our new line.	A.B.C

WAR DIARY
or
INTELLIGENCE SUMMARY.
(Erase heading not required.)

Army Form C. 2118.

Instructions regarding War Diaries and Intelligence Summaries are contained in F. S. Regs., Part II. and the Staff Manual respectively. Title pages will be prepared in manuscript.

Place	Date	Hour	Summary of Events and Information	Remarks and references to Appendices
	29th		No Infantry action in our Sector during the day although Enemy shelling was heavy throughout.	
HANGARD	30th		The Battalion withdrew to rest to HANGARD WOOD. Orders were received to prepare to Counter-attack. Half an hour later the Battalion moved forward and attacked to restore NORTH of HANGARD WOOD and forced the Enemy to retire causing him very heavy Casualties. The Battalion dug in with extreme difficulty under heavy shell and Machine Gun fire. A heavy Enemy attack formed our flanks and the Battalion reassembled and attacked again (under 2nd Lieut. G. POWELL) regaining the same position and capturing an Enemy Machine Gun which was turned upon the Enemy. Our left was again driven in by an Enemy attack and the Battalion again fell back. The Battalion again Counter-attacked with 2nd Lieut. G. POWELL in Command and the position were again regained. The Battalion was relieved. Heavy Casualties.	
LONGNEU	31st		No Infantry actions took place. The Battalion was relieved by ANZAC troops and proceeded to billets at LONGNEU.	

WAR DIARY
or
INTELLIGENCE SUMMARY.
(Erase heading not required.)

Army Form C. 2118.

Place	Date	Hour	Summary of Events and Information	Remarks and references to Appendices
			Casualties from March 21st - March 31st were as follows:-	
			Lieut Col. J.R. WEBSTER DSO MC. Missing 22-3-18	
			Major H.R. STEVENS. MC Wounded 24.3.18.	
			Captain L.J.B. HARRISON Killed in action 27-3-18	
			Captain T.C.O. WILLIAMS MC Wounded 24-3-18	
			(Died of Wounds 27-3-18)	
			Lieut F.H. GOSLING MC Wounded 22-3-18	
			Lieut C.E. GARLAND " 28-3-18	
			Lieut R.C. DAVIES MC " 31-3-18	
			Lieut R.M. DRYNAN " 31-3-18	
			Lieut G. REECE " 22-3-18	
			2nd Lieut. C.E. ROBINSON " 31-3-18	
			2nd Lieut. E.E. WILSON " 22.3.18	
			2nd Lieut. R.N. BARKER " 23-3-18	
			2nd Lieut. C.E. ALLEN " 22-3-18	
			2nd Lieut. A.G. HOLLOWAY Killed in action 24.3.18	

WAR DIARY
INTELLIGENCE SUMMARY

Army Form C. 2118.

Places	Date	Hour	Summary of Events and Information	Remarks and references to Appendices
			Casualties Continued:-	21
			2nd Lieut. W.H. Foxon. Wounded 31-3-18.	
			2nd Lieut. H. Drabble " 24-3-18	
			2nd Lieut. G.E. Wood " 21-3-18	
			2nd Lieut. C.H. Rollason " 30-3-18	
			2nd Lieut. N.S. Dye Wounded & Missing 20-3-18	W.C.K.
			2nd Lieut. H.B. Busnell " 31-3-18	
			2nd Lieut. F. Nurse Missing 20-3-18	W.C.K.
			OTHER RANKS:- 114 Killed. 104 Missing. 179 Wounded.	

Harry Lewis Lieut Col.
Commanding 16th Battalion Sherwood Foresters.

16th Bn. Sherwood Foresters.

WAR DIARY

INTELLIGENCE SUMMARY

No 27

Place	Date	Hour	Summary of Events and Information	Remarks and references to Appendices
RECQUES	MAY 1918 1st.		Working Parties were found for constructing Training Grounds for American Units	M/S.B
	2nd		ditto	M/S.B
	3rd		ditto	M/S.B
	4th		ditto	M/S.B
	5th		ditto	M/S.B
	6th		2/Lieut. G. POWELL and 130 OTHER RANKS rejoined the Battalion from No 3. Composite Battalion.	1/S.B
	7th		The Transport Section rejoined the Battalion from No 3. Composite Battalion. Captain W.H.L. BULKELEY transferred to 15th Bn Sherwood Foresters. Cleaning up and reorganisation.	2/S.B 26A
	8th		Information having been received from General Headquarters that a Battalion Training Staff would	M/S.B

WAR DIARY

INTELLIGENCE SUMMARY

Army Form C. 2118.

Place	Date	Hour	Summary of Events and Information	Remarks and references to Appendices
RECQUES	MAY 8th (cont)		be formed from the Battalion for the purpose of training American Units and surplus personnel despatched to the Base. Officers, Warrant Officers, N.C.O's and men were selected to form the Training Staff.	
	9th		Training was carried out. The "Judies" Concert Party gave a concert to all men who returned from No. 3 Composite Battalion.	W.C.B.
	10th		Surplus Personnel were organised ready for Drafts.	W.C.B.
	11th		Training was carried out.	W.C.B.
	12th		do	W.C.B.
	13th		do	W.C.B.
	14th		Battalion Sports held. The G.O.C. 117th Infantry Brigade was in attendance.	W.C.B.

WAR DIARY
INTELLIGENCE SUMMARY.
(Erase heading not required.)

Army Form C. 2118.

Instructions regarding War Diaries and Intelligence Summaries are contained in F. S. Regs., Part II. and the Staff Manual respectively. Title pages will be prepared in manuscript.

Place	Date	Hour	Summary of Events and Information	Remarks and references to Appendices
	MAY			
RECQUES	14th		2/Lieut. L. SURRIDGE, 2/Lieut. W.G. WHITWORTH and 10 N.C.O. Instructors proceeded with No.1 Battn. 307th Infantry Regiment, A.E.F. to III Army Area.	W.6.B.
	15th		117th Brigade Horse Show was held at ZUTKERQUE. Capt. R.W. ILLINGWORTH. D.S.O. M.C. and 9 N.C.O. Instructors proceeded with 3rd Battn. 307th Infantry Regiment A.E.F. to III Army Area.	W.6.B.
	16th		Surplus Personnel consisting of 232 OTHER RANKS proceeded to ETAPLES for posting to other Units, entraining at AUDRUICQ at 10.a.m.	W.6.B.
	17th		Surplus Transports and 38 OTHER RANKS proceeded to CUCQ by march route. Lt. Col. J.S. CASSY, M.C. proceeded to act as Umpire at 77th Division (A.E.F.) Manoeuvres at WATTEN.	W.6.B.
	19th		Church Parade Service in the MILL RECQUES. Lt. Col. J.S. CASSY, M.C. rejoined the Battalion.	W.6.B.
	20th		The Battalion played the 10th Depot A.O.C. at football at AUDRUICQ. Result, 1 goal each.	W.6.B.

WAR DIARY
INTELLIGENCE SUMMARY.
(Erase heading not required.)

Army Form C. 2118.

Place	Date	Hour	Summary of Events and Information	Remarks and references to Appendices
RECQUES	MAY. 21st		Training of N.C.O's forming part of the Battalion Training Staff	
	22nd		— ditto —	
	23rd		A further draft of 38 OTHER RANKS proceeded to ETAPLES. The Training Staff proceeded to the MENTQUE Area by march route. The following decorations were awarded to the undermentioned for gallantry and devotion to duty:- BAR TO MILITARY MEDAL. 70362. Pte. W. RAYMENT. M.M. MILITARY MEDAL. 21749. Sergt. W. SHAW. 71482. Pte. A.E. BARKER	
MENTQUE	24th		15 OTHER RANKS proceeded to GUEMY to form the Rifle Grenade Section of the 39th Divisional Demonstration Platoon. Draft of 9 OTHER RANKS proceeded to ETAPLES.	
	25th		Capt. R.L. ILLINGWORTH. D.S.O., M.C., 2/Lieut. L. SURRIDGE 2/Lieut. W.C. WHITWORTH and 19 N.C.O. Instructors returned from 307th Infantry Regiment, A.E.F.	

WAR DIARY
INTELLIGENCE SUMMARY

Army Form C. 2118.

Place	Date	Hour	Summary of Events and Information	Remarks and references to Appendices
MENTQUE.	MAY. 26th.		Billets &c. were arranged for the arrival of the 117th Regt. 30th A.E.F. Division. The following decorations were awarded to the undermentioned for gallantry and devotion to duty:—	M.G.B.
			MILITARY MEDAL. 200184. C.S.M. J. ILIFFE. 26523. Sergt. F. MORLEY.	
			66601. 2/Cpl. J.S. FOSTER. 70036. 2/Lt. T. REYNOLDS.	
			21560. 2/Cpl. L. HEWITT. 21621. 2/Cpl. W. LEES.	
			MENTIONED IN DESPATCHES. 27508 Sergt. C. SLACK.	
	27th		The 30th American Division arrived and the 1st and 3rd Battns. of the 117th Regt were affiliated to the Battn. for training purposes. The former Battn. were billeted at MENTQUE and the latter at INGLINGHEM.	M.G.B.
	28th.		Capt. R.L. ILLINGWORTH, D.S.O., M.C. proceeded for attachment to the 17th K.R.R.C.	M.G.B.
	29th.		American Battns. commenced training	M.G.B.
	30th.		Capt. W.E. WRIGHT, M.C. joined the Battalion from 2nd Bn. Sherwood Foresters.	M.G.B.

WAR DIARY

INTELLIGENCE SUMMARY

Army Form C. 2118.

Place	Date	Hour	Summary of Events and Information	Remarks and references to Appendices
MENTRUE	MAY 31st		Training was carried out.	M.L.R.
	JUNE 1st. 1918			

Maley Lieut. Col.,
Comdg 10th Battn Sherwood Foresters

16 N'olk 7 Datal 39

Army Form C. 2118.

WAR DIARY
or
INTELLIGENCE SUMMARY.
(Erase heading not required.)

Vol 28

Place	Date	Hour	Summary of Events and Information	Remarks and references to Appendices
MENTQUE	JUNE 1st	1918	Training was carried out.	W.B.B
	2nd			
	3rd		The following decorations were awarded to the undermentioned Officers & N.C.Os for gallantry during operations March 21st to 31st/1918. The Distinguished Service Order.	W.B.B
			2ND LIEUT. G. POWELL.	
			Bar to Military Medal	
			NO 26842. C.S.M. B. WALKER M.M.	
			2/395. SERGT. J. PAGE M.M.	
	4th		NO. 27508. SERGEANT C. SLACK "Mentioned in Despatches" in the King's Birthday Honours. Training was carried out.	27A

WAR DIARY
or
INTELLIGENCE SUMMARY.

Army Form C. 2118.

Place	Date	Hour	Summary of Events and Information	Remarks and references to Appendices
MENIN QUE	JUNE 5th		The following men received Officerations cards from Major General C.A Blacklock C.M.G. D.S.O. Comdg 39th Division for their great courage during operations March 21st to 31st /1918.	W.E.B
			NO. RANK NAME	
			26561. PTE. F BAINES	
			92081. " W. MARTIN	
			50194 " A.G. MOORES	
			The following Officers granted the acting rank of Captain.	
			LIEUT. M.A ELLISSEN. M.C. 2ND LT. W.E. BOSWELL 2ND LT. G. POWELL. D.S.O. 2ND LT. L. SURRIDGE	
			2ND LT. E.V. SMALLEY.	
			Training was carried out.	
	6:		CAPTAIN A. KERR posted to 10th BN. SHERWOOD FORESTERS and struck off strength accordingly	W.E.B
			Training was carried out.	

Army Form C. 2118.

WAR DIARY
or
INTELLIGENCE SUMMARY.
(Erase heading not required.)

Instructions regarding War Diaries and Intelligence Summaries are contained in F. S. Regs., Part II. and the Staff Manual respectively. Title pages will be prepared in manuscript.

Place	Date	Hour	Summary of Events and Information	Remarks and references to Appendices
MENTQUE	JUNE. 7th		LIEUT. E.S. EGAN. MORC (American Expeditionary Force) Medical Officer attached to the Battalion, proceeded to join 36th Division	W.E.B.
	8th		CAPTAIN E.V. SMALLEY rejoined the Battalion from a course.	W.E.B.
	9th		CAPTAIN M.A. ELLISSEN M.C. posted to 1ST BN SHERWOOD FORESTERS and struck off strength accordingly. Training was carried out.	W.E.B.
	10th		— ditto — Divine Service was held.	
	11th		} Training was carried out.	W.E.B.
	12th			
	13th			
	14th		CAPTAIN E.V. SMALLEY proceeded on 14 days leave to ENGLAND.	W.E.B.
	15th		} Training was carried out.	
	16th		Training was carried out.	W.E.B.

WAR DIARY
INTELLIGENCE SUMMARY
(Erase heading not required.)

Army Form C. 2118.

Place	Date	Hour	Summary of Events and Information	Remarks and references to Appendices
MENIN QUE.	JUNE 17th			
	18th		Training was carried out.	W.E.B.
	19th			
	20th			
	21st		Training was carried out	W.E.B.
			Rev. J.F. BLOXAM M.C. proceeded on 14 days leave to ENGLAND	
			CAPTAIN W.E. WRIGHT M.C. proceeded to 111 Bde HQrs as Acting Staff Captain	
	22nd		Training was carried out	W.E.B.
			CAPTAIN R.L. ILLINGWORTH D.S.O. M.C. rejoined the Battalion from 14 K.R.R.C.	
	23rd		Training was carried out	W.E.B.
	24th		QUARTERMASTER & HON. LIEUT. A. HOWLETT joined the Battalion for duty	
	25th		Training was carried out.	W.E.B.
	26th		The 30th AMERICAN DIVISION ascended orders to move at short notice to the CASSEL Sector of the WINNEZEELE Line, accompanied by officers of British Training Units. The Battalion would proceed with 1st & 3rd Battns 114 Regt & Battn Headqrs with 114th American Regt. Headqrs.	

Army Form C. 2118.

WAR DIARY
or
INTELLIGENCE SUMMARY.
(Erase heading not required.)

Places	Date	Hour	Summary of Events and Information	Remarks and references to Appendices
MENTQUE	JUNE 26th		BRIGADIER GENERAL G.A ARMITAGE C.M.G D.S.O. the staff of 14 Brigade Judges proceeded to SAMER to take over the supervision of the training of the 30th American Division. LIEUT. COL. C.H.N. SEYMOUR D.SO Comdg 14 KRRC took over command of the Brigade	W.T.G.B.
	27th		Training was carried out	
	28th			
	29th		Training was carried out	W.T.G.B.
	30th		Rest.	W.T.G.B.

Comdg 16 Bn Sherwood Foresters
[signature] Lieut Colonel

Army Form C. 2118.

WAR DIARY
or
INTELLIGENCE SUMMARY.
(Erase heading not required.)

Place	Date	Hour	Summary of Events and Information	Remarks and references to Appendices
	June 3rd/18		Appendix "A"	
			The following telegram was sent to EQUERRY BUCKINGHAM PALACE by BRIGADIER GENERAL G A ARMYTAGE CMG DSO Comdg 114 Infantry Brigade.	W.E.B.
			"All ranks 114th Infantry Brigade offer congratulations to HIS MAJESTY on the occasion of his birthday."	
			The following reply was received by BRIGADIER GENERAL G A ARMYTAGE CMG DSO from EQUERRY BUCKINGHAM PALACE.	
			"The King much appreciates the good wishes of the 114th Infantry Brigade and His Majesty thanks all ranks for their congratulations."	

WAR DIARY
or
INTELLIGENCE SUMMARY.

16 Notts & Derby

Place	Date	Hour	Summary of Events and Information	Remarks and references to Appendices
	1916			
MENTQUE	JULY 1st		Training was carried out. Captain E.V. SMALLEY rejoined the Battalion from leave in England.	
	2nd.		The 30th American Division proceeded to II Corps Area. Lt. Col. J.S. CASEY, M.C. proceeded with 1/117 Regt and Capt. R.L. ILLINGWORTH, D.S.O., M.C. with 3/117 Regt.	
	4th.		Lt. Col. J.S. CASEY, M.C. rejoined the Battalion from 1/117 Regt. A.E.F.	
	5th.		A shooting competition on the 30 yard Range at MENTQUE was held between the Officers and N.C.O's who were attached to the 1st Bn and those who were attached to the 3rd Bn 117 Regt. A.E.F. resulting in a win for the former.	
	6th.		Capt. R.L. ILLINGWORTH, D.S.O., M.C. rejoined the Battn from the 3rd Bn. 117 Regt. A.E.F. Capt. G. POWELL, D.S.O. and Capt. L. SURRIDGE proceeded for attachment to 117 Regt. A.E.F. Revd. J.F. BLOXAM, M.C. rejoined the Bn. from leave in England.	28A
	7th.		Church Service was held.	

Army Form C. 2118.

WAR DIARY
INTELLIGENCE SUMMARY.
(Erase heading not required.)

Instructions regarding War Diaries and Intelligence Summaries are contained in F.S. Regs., Part II. and the Staff Manual respectively. Title pages will be prepared in manuscript.

Place	Date	Hour	Summary of Events and Information	Remarks and references to Appendices
MENTQUE.	JULY 8TH		Appreciation cards were received from Major General C.A. BLACKLOCK, C.M.G., D.S.O. for the undermentioned Officers, W.O.'s, N.C.O.'s and Men for their gallantry and devotion to duty during the dates stated March 21st to 31st 1918.	W66
			Capt. R.L. ILLINGWORTH, D.S.O., M.C. Capt. G. POWELL, D.S.O.	
			26842 C.S.M. B. WALKER. 200184 C.S.M. J. ILLIFFE. 70036 2/Lt. T. REYNOLDS. 65801 2/Lt. J.S. FOSTER.	
			70362 Pte. W. RAYMENT. 26621 2/Lt. W. LEES. 10954 Sgt. A. ADAMS. 26523 Sgt. F. MORLEY. 215 2/Lt. L. HEWITT.	
			April 17th to 20th 1918.	
			Capt. C. CLAYTON, M.C.	
			21749. Sergt. W. SHAW. 71428. Pte. A.E. PARKER.	
	10TH.		Capt. R.L. ILLINGWORTH, D.S.O., M.C. proceeded to ALDERSHOT to attend a course of Instruction at the Senior Officers School.	W66
	13TH		A shooting competition was held on the 30 yards Rifle Range at LA GRAND MARNIER between 12 W.O.'s and N.C.O.'s of the Battn. and 12 W.O.'s and N.C.O.'s of the 17th K.R.R.C. resulting in an easy win for the former. The scores were as follows:- 16th Sherwood Foresters 0931	W66

WAR DIARY

INTELLIGENCE SUMMARY.

Army Form C. 2118.

Place	Date	Hour	Summary of Events and Information	Remarks and references to Appendices
MENTQUE	JULY 13TH		17th K.R.R.C. 842. Maximum 1260. 2/Lt. B.C.B. WILES proceeded to 39th Div. H.Q for temporary duty as Divisional Gas Officer	MB
	14TH.		Divine Service was held	MB
	15TH.		A shooting competition was held on the 30 yards Rifle Range at INGLINGHEM between 12 W.O's and N.C.O's of the Battn. and 12. W.O's and N.C.O's of the 16th Rifle Brigade resulting in an easy win for the former. The scores were as follows:- 16th Sherwood Foresters 1143. 16th Rifle Brigade 869. Maximum Points 1320.	MB
	16TH.		The following Officers were attached to the 118th Infantry Brigade to take part in a Tactical Exercise under Brig. Gen A.B. HUBBACK Cmdg. 118th Brigade - Lt Col J.S. CASSY, M.C. Capt. W.E. BOSWELL, Capt E.V. SMALLEY and 2/Lieut W.C. WHITWORTH	MB
	18TH		2/Lieut B.C.B. WILES rejoined the Battalion from 39th Division	MB

WAR DIARY
INTELLIGENCE SUMMARY.
(Erase heading not required.)

Army Form C. 2118.

Place	Date	Hour	Summary of Events and Information	Remarks and references to Appendices
MENTQUE	JULY 19TH		Capt. G. POWELL, D.S.O. and Capt. L. SURRIDGE rejoined the Battn. from 117 Rgt. B.E.F.	W.6.B
	20TH		2/Lieut W.C. WHITWORTH proceeded to 2nd Army Central School, WISQUES to attend a months Infantry Course.	W.6.B
	21ST		Divine Service was held.	W.6.B
	25TH		The Battn. proceeded by march route from MENTQUE and took over billets at NORDAUSQUES.	W.6.B
NORDAUSQUES	26TH		2/Lt. Col. J.S. CASSY, M.C., Capt. G. POWELL, D.S.O. and 2/Lieut. B.C.B. WILES proceeded to CAMIERS to attend a demonstration of Machine Gun Barrage at the Machine Gun School	W.6.B
	27TH		The 117th Bde. H.Qrs. returned from SAMER and were established at RECQUES.	W.6.B
	28TH		Divine Service was held.	W.6.B

WAR DIARY
or
INTELLIGENCE SUMMARY

Army Form C. 2118.

Place	Date	Hour	Summary of Events and Information	Remarks and references to Appendices
NORDAUSQUES	29TH		Capt. L. SURRIDGE and 2/Lieut. B.C.B. WILES proceeded to attend courses at 2nd Army Musketry School. Lieut. Col. J.S. CASSY, M.C. proceeded on leave to PARIS. 20683 Sergt. S.A. STYCH proceeded to England for temporary commission. CAPTAIN G POWELL DSO assumed temporary command of the Battalion vice Lieut Col. J.S. Cassy M.C.	W695

G Powell Capt.
Comdg 16th Bn Sherwood Foresters

[Stamp: (3) BATTN. SHERWOOD FORESTERS ORDERLY ROOM 31.7.18]

66TH DIVISION
TRAINING CADRES

39 DIV

16TH BN SHERWOOD FORESTERS
~~Aug   1918~~

1918 AUG   1919 JUNE

~~[sketch]~~   39 DIV
           117 Bde

Served with 197 Bde
L of C fm Sept 1918

CONFIDENTIAL

WAR DIARY

OF

16th Bn. SHERWOOD FORESTERS.

From August 1st., 1918. To August 31st., 1918.

(Volume 3)

Army Form C. 2118.

WAR DIARY
INTELLIGENCE SUMMARY.
(Erase heading not required.)

Place	Date	Hour	Summary of Events and Information	Remarks and references to Appendices
NORDAUSQUES	August. 1.		The Battalion played the 117th Brigade in the 1st Round of the 39th Division Knock-out Tournament resulting in a win for the latter. The scores were :- 117 Brigade 72. 16th Sherwood Foresters 36	
	2.		The Battalion played the 39th Divl Signal Coy in the Final of the 39th Divisional Football Competition resulting in a win for the former by 4 goals to nil. Brig. Gen. A.B.HUBBACK, C.M.G., Condg. 118th Brigade presented the Cup and Medals after the game. The following Officer W.O., N.C.O.'s and men represented the Battalion :- Capt. G. POWELL, D.S.O., 26842 C.S.M. B. WALKER, M.M., 25699 C.Q.M.S. A.G.HILDRETH, D.C.M. 29777 Sgt. E. GILLATT, 26718 Sgt. T. CAVILL, 26419 Pte. B. CARSON, 6889 Pte. W.E.ROPER, 26561 Pte. F. BAINES, 28089 Pte. P. FELSTEAD, 92055 Pte. E.H. MORLEY, 27668 Pte. A.E. GOODWIN.	
	4.		Divine Service was held.	
	5.		Capt. E.V. SMALLEY proceeded to attend a Course of Instruction at VII Corps Schools.	
	7.		Lieut. & Qr. Mr. A. HOLLETT proceeded on leave to England.	

Army Form C. 2118.

WAR DIARY
or
INTELLIGENCE SUMMARY.
(Erase heading not required.)

Place	Date	Hour	Summary of Events and Information	Remarks and references to Appendices
	August			
NORDAUSQUES	8.		Lieut. Col. J.S. CASSY, M.C. returned from leave in Paris and assumed command of the Battalion. A shooting competition was held on the 30yds Rifle Range at LA GRAND MARNIER between 12 Officers, W.O's and N.C.O.'s of the Battn. and 12 Officers, W.O's and N.C.O.'s of the 17th K.R.R.C. resulting in an easy win for the former. The scores were:- 16th Sherwood Foresters 1674 - 17th K.R.R.C. 1387.	
	9.		The Battn. played the A.O.C., AUDRUICQ DEPOT, at football, resulting in a draw of 2 goals each.	
	11.		2/Lieut B.C.B. WILES proceeded to 15 Corps Schools as a Musketry Instructor.	
	13.		Capt B.W.E. WRIGHT, M.C. rejoined the Battn. from 117th Brigade Headquarters.	
	15.		The 117th Brigade were transferred to Lines of Communication. 117Bde.H.Q. proceeded to ROUEN and the Battn. proceeded by rail from NORTKERQUE to ABANCOURT coming under the orders of MAJOR GENERAL H.K. BETHELL, C.M.G., D.S.O., Comdg. 66th Division. Capt. G. POWELL D.S.O. proceeded on leave to England. Revd. J.F. BLOXAM, M.C. was transferred to the 100th Infantry Brigade, 33rd Division.	

Army Form C. 2118.

WAR DIARY
or
INTELLIGENCE SUMMARY.
(Erase heading not required.)

Place	Date	Hour	Summary of Events and Information	Remarks and references to Appendices
	AUGUST			
ABANCOURT	16.		The Battalion arrived at ABANCOURT and were accommodated under canvas about 3 miles from the town, being affiliated to 198th Inf. Bde. commanded by Brig. Gen. A.J. HUNTER, D.S.O, M.C.	
	17		Capt. W.E. BOSWELL proceeded to England on leave.	
	18		268142 C.S.M. B. WALKER, M.M. proceeded to England for a Commission.	
	19		28128 Sergt. A.E. SUMMERS. do	
	20		71130 Sergt. E. EGERTON, V.C. do	
	21		Capt. L. SURRIDGE rejoined the Battn. from attending a course at 2nd Army Musketry School.	
QUESNES.	23.		The Battn. proceeded to QUESNES Camp near HAUDRICOURT by march route and were accommodated under canvas.	
	25.		Lieut. & Qr. Mr. A. HOLLETT rejoined the Battn. from leave to England. 2/Lieut. W.C. WHITWORTH rejoined the Battn. from course at 2ND Army Central School.	

Army Form C. 2118.

WAR DIARY
INTELLIGENCE SUMMARY.

(Erase heading not required.)

Instructions regarding War Diaries and Intelligence Summaries are contained in F. S. Regs., Part II. and the Staff Manual respectively. Title pages will be prepared in manuscript.

Place	Date	Hour	Summary of Events and Information	Remarks and references to Appendices
	AUGUST			
QUESNES.	27.		Lieut. Col. J.S. CASSY, M.C. proceeded on leave to Paris. Capt. W.E. WRIGHT, M.C. assuming temporary command of the Battalion.	
	29.		The Battalion played the 7th Suffolk Regt. at football and won the scores being 5-3.	
	30.		Capt. L. SURRIDGE proceeded to attend a months course at Fourth Army Musketry School.	
	31.		Lieut. Col. J.S. CASSY, M.C. returned from leave to Paris and assumed command of the Battalion.	

31st August, 1918.

Cassy Lieut. Col.,
Comdg 16th Bn. Sherwood Foresters

CONFIDENTIAL

WAR DIARY

OF

16th. SHERWOOD FORESTERS.

From 1st. September 1918. to 30th. September 1918.

Army Form C. 2118.

WAR DIARY
or
INTELLIGENCE SUMMARY
(Erase heading not required.)

Vol 31

Place	Date	Hour	Summary of Events and Information	Remarks and references to Appendices
QUESNES	SEPT. 1918. 1ST	—	Divine Service was held. 2/Lieut. W.C. WHITWORTH proceeded on leave to England. Capt. E.V. SMALLEY rejoined the Battalion from course at VII Corps School. R.S.M. J. PEPPER, M.C., proceeded on leave to England on the expiration of which he has to report to 'K' I.B.D. CALAIS owing to age. He has been the R.S.M. of the Battalion since its formation.	116
	3RD.		Capt. W.E. BOSWELL rejoined the Battalion from leave to England. The Battalion played the 7TH SUFFOLK REGT. at football and won, the scores being 4 – 1.	116
	4TH		Capt. W.E. WRIGHT, M.C. proceeded on leave to England. Under authority granted by His Majesty the King the Field Marshal Commanding in Chief has awarded the following decoration to the undermentioned N.C.O.'s for devotion to duty :- MERITORIOUS SERVICE MEDAL. 26079 C.Q.M.S. S. PARSONS. 6907 SGT. J. ROWAN.	116
	5TH		Capt. G. POWELL, D.S.O. rejoined the Battalion from leave to England.	116

Army Form C. 2118.

WAR DIARY
or
INTELLIGENCE SUMMARY.
(Erase heading not required.)

Instructions regarding War Diaries and Intelligence Summaries are contained in F. S. Regs., Part II, and the Staff Manual respectively. Title pages will be prepared in manuscript.

Place	Date	Hour	Summary of Events and Information	Remarks and references to Appendices
QUESNES.	8TH		Divine Service was held.	W.6.B
	11TH		2/Lt. B.C.B WILES absorbed into the Establishment of XV Corps School as Instructor.	W.6.B
	13TH		Capt. P.J. KELLY, R.A.M.C. attached to the Battalion for duties as Medical Officer.	W.6.B
	16TH		Capt. R.L. ILLINGWORTH, D.S.O., M.C., struck off strength of the Battalion, being in hospital sick in England.	W.6.B
	17TH		The Battalion played the 18th N.F.'s at football, and lost, the score being 1 - O.	W.6.B
	18TH		Eight O.R.'s of the R.W.F.'s joined the Battalion for attachment. 2/Lieut. W.G.WHITWORTH rejoined the Battalion from leave to England.	W.6.B
	19TH		Under authority granted by His Majesty the King, the Field Marshal Commanding in Chief has awarded the M.S.M. to No.27701 Sgt. A.A. COBB for devotion to duty.	W.6.B

WAR DIARY
of
INTELLIGENCE SUMMARY.
(Erase heading not required.)

Army Form C. 2118.

Place	Date	Hour	Summary of Events and Information	Remarks and references to Appendices
QUESNES	21st		The Battalion came under the orders of 197th Infantry Brigade commanded by Brig. Gen. L.L. WHEATLEY, C.M.G., D.S.O.	W&B
	22nd		Capt. W.E. WRIGHT, M.C., rejoined the Battalion from leave to England.	W&B
	24th		The following Officers and O.R's joined the Battalion for attachment :- Lieut. J.B. O'FARREL and 2/Lieut. T.G.B. SUTHERLAND ROYAL MUNSTER FUSILIERS. 35 O.R. 7th Bn. S.W.B. 40 O.R. 2nd Bn. D.C.L.I. 1 O.R. 1/5th DEVON REGT. 60 " 8th Bn. S.W.B. 31 " 8th Bn. D.C.L.I 25 O.R. 12th HAMPSHIRE REGT.	W&B
	25th		The following joined the Battalion for attachment :- 18 O.R. SUFFOLK REGT. 7 O.R. BUFFS REGT. 1 O.R. HANTS. 1 O.R. NORFOLKS. 48 O.R. MIDDLESEX REGT.	W&B
	26th		Lieut. Col. J.S. CASSY, M.C. proceeded on leave to England. Captain W.E WRIGHT, M.C., assumed temporary command of the Battalion.	W&B

WAR DIARY
INTELLIGENCE SUMMARY.
(Erase heading not required.)

Army Form C. 2118.

Place	Date	Hour	Summary of Events and Information	Remarks and references to Appendices
QUESNES.	27TH	-	The following joined the Battalion for attachment:-	W.B.B.
			12. O.R's. SUFFOLK REGT. 8. O.R's MIDDLESEX 24. O.R' BUFFS. REGT.	
			4. O.R' HANTS REGT. 5. O.R' S.W.B.	
	29TH		Divine Service was held. Capt. L. SURRIDGE rejoined the Battalion from attending Course at 4TH Army Infantry School.	W.B.B.

W.E. Wright Captain,
Comdg. 16th Bn. Sherwood Foresters.

1st OCTOBER, 1918.

CONFIDENTIAL.

WAR DIARY.

of

16th. Bn. SHERWOOD FORESTERS.

From 1ST OCTOBER, 1918.   To 31st. OCTOBER, 1918.

Army Form C. 2118.

WAR DIARY
INTELLIGENCE SUMMARY.
(Erase heading not required.)

Place	Date	Hour	Summary of Events and Information	Remarks and references to Appendices
QUESNES.	OCTOBER 2ND.		6709b. C.S.M. W. ARKINSTALL, D.C.M., rejoined the Battalion from 'K' I.B.D.	
	4TH.		Lt. J.B. O'FARRELL and 2/Lt. T.G.B. SUTHERLAND, R.M.F's attached to the Battalion, left to join the 6th R.D.F's.	
	5TH.		The Battalion played the 25th N.F's in the first round of the Football League for London Staffs, and won, the scores being 5-1.	
	6TH.		Divine Service was held. Brig. Gen. J.H. HALL, C.M.G., D.S.O. assumed command of the Brigade.	
	7TH.		Battalion Cross-Country race was held.	
	8TH.		Captain W.E. BOSWELL admitted to Field Ambulance, sick.	
	11TH.		The following joined the Battalion for attachment :— 2. O.R's. S.W.B's. 2. O.R's. MIDD'X R. 1. O.R. BEDFORD R. 8. O.R's. DEVON R. 9. O.R's. BUFFS. 9. O.R's HANTS R. 2. O.R's. SOMERSET L.I.	

Army Form C. 2118.

WAR DIARY
INTELLIGENCE SUMMARY.
(Erase heading not required.)

Instructions regarding War Diaries and Intelligence Summaries are contained in F. S. Regs., Part II. and the Staff Manual respectively. Title pages will be prepared in manuscript.

Place	Date	Hour	Summary of Events and Information	Remarks and references to Appendices
QUESNES.	OCTOBER 12TH.		The Battalion played the 13TH GLOUCESTER REGT. in the Cadre League at football, and won :- 4 - 1.	
	13TH.		LT. COL. J.S. CASSY, M.C., rejoined the Battalion from leave to England and assumed command of the Battalion. CAPT. W.E. BOSWELL rejoined from hospital.	
	14TH.		A/R.S.M. A. COKAYNE, D.C.M., reverted to C.S.M., and ordered to report to "K" I.B.D. CALAIS. C.S.M. W. ARKINSTALL, D.C.M., appointed A/R.S.M.	
	18TH.		The Battalion played the 13th GLOUCESTER REGT. at Rugby, and won by 13 POINTS - NIL.	
	19TH.		The Battalion played the 16TH RIFLE BRIGADE in the Cadre League at football, and made a draw.	
	20TH.		The following joined the Battalion for attachment :- 3. O.R's MIDD'X R., 5. O.R's SUFFOLKS R., 11. O.R's BUFFS. 5. O.R's S.W.B's. 8. O.R's HANTS. 2. O.R's D.C.L.I. 5.O.R's DEVON R.	
	24TH		The following men attached to the Battalion were transferred to Battalions as under :-	

WAR DIARY
INTELLIGENCE SUMMARY

Army Form C. 2118.

Place	Date	Hour	Summary of Events and Information	Remarks and references to Appendices
QUESNES	OCTOBER 24TH (CONT..)		55. O.Rs. S.W.B's TRANSFERRED TO 7TH WILTS. R. 5. O.Rs. BUFFS TRANSFERRED TO 3RD. R.Fs. 32. O.Rs. D.C.L.I. " " 15. O.Rs. SUFFOLKS " " 15. O.Rs. HANTS " " 23. O.Rs. MIDDLESEX " " 1. O.R. NORFOLK " "	
	26TH		CAPT. L. SURRIDGE proceeded on leave to England. The Battalion played the 10TH LINCOLNS in the Entire League at Football and won :- 3-1. 2/LT. W.T.J. RUMSEY 1ST. EAST SURREYS joined the Battalion for attachment.	
	27TH		Divine Service was held. CAPT. P.J. KELLY, R.A.M.C. proceeded to No.1. L.of C. DETENTION HOSPITAL for duty.	
	29TH		Boxing Tournament was held in the afternoon.	

1ST NOVEMBER, 1918.

[signature] Lt. Col.

CMDG. 16TH BN. SHERWOOD FORESTERS.

CONFIDENTIAL.

WAR DIARY

OF

16th. Battalion SHERWOOD FORESTERS.

From :- 1st. Novr. 1918.   To :- 30th. Novr. 1918.

Army Form C. 2118.

WAR DIARY
or
INTELLIGENCE SUMMARY.
(Erase heading not required.)

Vol 33

Instructions regarding War Diaries and Intelligence Summaries are contained in F. S. Regs., Part II. and the Staff Manual respectively. Title pages will be prepared in manuscript.

Place	Date	Hour	Summary of Events and Information	Remarks and references to Appendices
QUESNES	NOVEMBER 1918 2ND.		162. O.R's (MALARIALS) joined for attachment	
	3RD.		Divine Service was held	
	8TH		56. O.R's transferred to Battalions as under :- 10. O.R's to 18TH KING'S LIVERPOOL REGT. 6. O.R's to 5TH ROYAL INNISKILLING FUS: 40. O.R's to 6TH R. DUBLIN F's	
	10TH		Divine Service was held. The Battalion played the 18TH NORTHUMBERLAND FUS: at football and won :- 2.0.	
	11TH		The Battalion played the 13TH GLOUCESTER REGT. at Rugby and won :- 6-5 points. The announcement of the signing of the Armistice with Germany was circulated to the Battalion at about 18.00 hrs and was received with vociferous cheering	
	12TH		Divine Service to commemorate the signing of the Armistice was held and was attended by all troops under the administration of 197th Infantry Brigade. Battalion Sports were held in the afternoon. The Battalion Band played selections at a Brigade Boxing Tournament in the evening	

Army Form C. 2118.

WAR DIARY
INTELLIGENCE SUMMARY.
(Erase heading not required.)

Instructions regarding War Diaries and Intelligence Summaries are contained in F. S. Regs., Part II. and the Staff Manual respectively. Title pages will be prepared in manuscript.

Place	Date	Hour	Summary of Events and Information	Remarks and references to Appendices
QUESNES	13th		2/Lt. H.L. Walker and 2/Lt J. McLean (A.& S.H's) joined for attachments	
	14th		2/Lt. W.A. Gracey and 2/Lt. G.T. Mair (Gordon H's) joined for attachment	
	15th		Capt. F.P. Grove, R.A.M.C. joined for attachment	
	17th		Divine Service was held.	
	19th		The Battalion won the Bde. Cross Country Run by 91 points. The Battalion played the 10th Lincoln Regt. in the final of the Bde Rugby Championship and lost	
	20th		The Battalion played the 23rd Northumberland Fus' at football and won :- 6. 1.	
	21st		Capt. G. Powell, D.S.O. and Capt. W.E. Boswell admitted to hospital. Capt. W.E. Wright, M.C. appointed Acting Adjutant	

Army Form C. 2118.

WAR DIARY
or
INTELLIGENCE SUMMARY.
(Erase heading not required.)

Place	Date	Hour	Summary of Events and Information	Remarks and references to Appendices
QUESNES	22nd		Major G.R. Mott, South Lancs Regt. joined for attachment. A Boxing Tournament was held in the evening	
	23rd		Bde Sports were held	
	24th		Divine Service was held	
	25th		94 O.R.'s were transferred to various Battalions	
	27th		Capt E.V. Smalley proceeded on leave to England	
	28th		Lieut Col. J.S. Cassy M.C. proceeded on leave to PARIS. Major G.R. Mott assumed command of the Battalion	
	30th		The Battalion Machine Gun Football team won the Championship of the Bde 'C' Football League.	

J.S. Cassy Major
Cmdg. 16th Bn Sherwood Foresters.

NOVEMBER 30th 1918.

Army Form C. 2118.

WAR DIARY
16th Battalion Sherwood Foresters.

INTELLIGENCE SUMMARY
(Erase heading not required.)

WO 34

Place	Date	Hour	Summary of Events and Information	Remarks and references to Appendices
Hautricourt Reinforcement Camp.	Dec:- 1st		Divine Service was held.	
	2nd		The Battalion played the 14th H.L.I. at football and won securing the Bde. Jug-of-War, competition for Lightweights of the Brigade League for Cadre Staffs. Captain L. Surridge rejoined from leave to England. Lt-Col. J.S. Cossey M.C. rejoined from leave to Paris.	
	3rd		The Battalion Hdrs. over the material personnel attached to 18th N.Fs, 23rd N.Fs & 14th H.L.I.	
	4th		The Band contributed selections at the Brigade Boxing Tournament.	
	5th		Divine Service was held. 72 O.Rs proceeded to Base Depôts.	
	9th		30 O.Rs proceeded to Base Depôts.	
	10th		10 O.Rs proceeded to Base Depôts.	
	11th		48 coalminers proceeded to Dieppe for Demobilisation.	
	12th		9 coalminers " " " "	
	13th		246 O.Rs left from various parties " "	
	14th		Capt. E.V. Smalley rejoined from leave to England.	
	15th		Divine Service was held.	
	16th		119 O.Rs proceeded to be Infant. Com: Camp.	
			50 " " " " Base Depôts	

Army Form C. 2118.

WAR DIARY
16th Sherwood Foresters
INTELLIGENCE SUMMARY

(Erase heading not required.)

Instructions regarding War Diaries and Intelligence Summaries are contained in F.S. Regs., Part II. and the Staff Manual respectively. Title pages will be prepared in manuscript.

Place	Date	Hour	Summary of Events and Information	Remarks and references to Appendices
Haudricourt Reinforcement Camp.	DEC. 20th		2/Lt. G. Jones proceeded to join 14th H.L.I. Capt. B. Bojoly proceeded to join 2.5th N.F.s. Lt-Col. J. Mackintosh joined the Battalion for attachment.	
	21st		Lt-Col. J.S. Cassy M.C. proceeded to take up appointment as Camp Commandant near Paris. Capt. W.E. Waugh M.C. assumed the duties of Commanding Officer vice Lt-Col. J.S. Cassy M.C. Capt. E.V. Smalley assumed the duties of Adjutant.	
	23rd		Lieut. A. Hollett proceeded on leave to England.	
	25th		The Battalion celebrated Christmas Day. A special Xmas dinner was held in mens dining hut. The band added greatly to the enjoyment of the festivities.	
	26th		The band proceeded to Aumale and gave selections in the Square.	
	27th		44 O.Rs left for various Battalions.	
	28th		12 O.Rs " " " "	
	29th		Divine service was held.	

C.E. Waugh Capt/Major
Commanding, 16th Batt. Sherwood Foresters.

Army Form C. 2118.

WAR DIARY
INTELLIGENCE SUMMARY.

(Erase heading not required.)

Instructions regarding War Diaries and Intelligence Summaries are contained in F. S. Regs., Part II. and the Staff Manual respectively. Title pages will be prepared in manuscript.

Place	Date	Hour	Summary of Events and Information	Remarks and references to Appendices
AUMALE.	1919. Jan.1st.		The Battalion moved into Billets in Aumale.	
	6th		Capt.W.E.Wright,M.C. and Capt.W.C.Whitworth proceeded on leave to England.	
	8th	2	33 Other Ranks left for various Battalions. 4 Other Ranks proceeded to LE TREPORT. 2 Other Ranks proceeded to join their Base Depots. Major H.R.Stevens,M.C. rejoined the Battalion from England.	
	9th		Lt.Col.J.S.Cassy,M.C. rejoined the Battalion.	
LE HAVRE.	15th		The Battalion comprised of 10 Officers and 52 Other Ranks proceeded to LE HAVRE and formed "C" Wing of the General Base Depot.	
	20th		2/Lt.J.McLean, proceeded to U.K. for Demobilisation.	
	22nd.		Capt.E.V.Smalley do do do do	
	23rd.		Capt.W.E.Wright,M.C. rejoined the Battalion.	
	24th		Lt.W.E.Boswell & Lieut.G.Powell,D.S.O. rejoined the Battalion from hospital.	
	29th.		2/Lt.G.T.Mair proceeded to U.K. for Demobilisation.	
	30th		Lt.A.Hellett rejoined from England and took over the duties of Camp Quartermaster.	
	31st.		Lt.Col.J.S.Cassy,M.C. proceeded to PARIS on leave.	

January 31st, 1919.

Lieut.Col.,
Cmdg.16th Bn.Sherwood Foresters.

Army Form C. 2118.

WAR DIARY
or
INTELLIGENCE SUMMARY

16th. Bn. Sherwood Foresters.
****

(Erase heading not required.)

Instructions regarding War Diaries and Intelligence Summaries are contained in F.S. Regs., Part II. and the Staff Manual respectively. Title pages will be prepared in manuscript.

Place	Date	Hour	Summary of Events and Information	Remarks and references to Appendices
	February.			
LE HAVRE.	4th.		Major H.R.Stevens, M.C. Assumed Command of the Battalion, during the absence of Lt.Col.J.S.Cassy.M.C. on Leave to England.	
do	4th.		Lt.Col.Bryne, Rifle Brigade., with his Staff took over from the Battalion the Administration of "C"Wing. General Base Depot.	
do	5th.		Lt.W.E.Boswell, proceeded to England for Demobilisation.	
do	7th.		Lt.J.C.T.Mackintosh, (Staffs. Yeo.) proceeded to England on Leave.	
do	12th.		Lt.& Qm.A.Hollett, was admitted to Hospital.	
do	14th.		Capt.L.Surridge, proceeded to England as Draft Conducting Officer.	
do	17th.		Lt.G.Powell. D.S.O., proceeded to the 8th. Bn.Sherwood Foresters on transfer.	
do	22nd.		Major H.R.Stevens,M.C. was admitted to Hospital.	
do	24th.		Capt.W.C.Whitworth, was admitted to Hospital.	
do	23rd.		Capt.W.E.Wright. M.C. Assumed Command of the Battalion, vice Major H.R.Stevens,M.C. to Hospital.	22/2/19

28/2/19.

W. E. Wright
Captain.
Cmdg. 16th. Sherwood Foresters.

Army Form C. 2118.

WAR DIARY
or
INTELLIGENCE SUMMARY
(Erase heading not required.)

16th. Bn. Sherwood Foresters.

Instructions regarding War Diaries and Intelligence Summaries are contained in F.S. Regs., Part II. and the Staff Manual respectively. Title pages will be prepared in manuscript.

Place	Date	Hour	Summary of Events and Information	Remarks and references to Appendices
1919. LE HAVRE.	MARCH. 1.	19/19	Lt. & Qm. A. Hollett, rejoined the Battalion from Hospital.	
do.	4th.		Capt. W.E. Wright, M.C. proceeded to 197th. Infantry Brigade, H.Q., to take over duties of Bde. Major.	
do.	5th.		Lt. J.C.T. Mackintosh, (Staffs Yeomanry) rejoined from leave to U.K.	
do.	6th.		Capt. L. Surridge, rejoined from leave to U.K.	
do.	7th.		Lt. J.C.T. Mackintosh. (Staffs. Yeomanry.) proceeded to England for Demobilisation.	
do.	9th.		Capt. W.C. Whitworth. rejoined the Battalion from Hospital.	
do.	9th.		Major H.R. Stevens, M.C. was evacuated to England from Hospital.	
do.	9th.		Capt. W.E. Wright, M.C. assumed Command of the Battalion, vice Major H.R. Stevens, M.C. to England.	
do.	9th.		Lt. Col. J.S. Cassy, M.C. was Demobilised whilst on leave to England, 26/2/1919.	
do.	19th.		Capt. L. Surridge. proceeded for attachment to M.L.O. HAVRE, for Cross Channel Transportation work.	

Captain.
Cmdg. 16th. Bn. Sherwood Foresters.

Army Form C. 2118.

WAR DIARY   APRIL 1919.
or
INTELLIGENCE SUMMARY.
(Erase heading not required.)

Place	Date	Hour	Summary of Events and Information	Remarks and references to Appendices
	3/4/1919.		Capt.L.Surridge, Capt.W.C.Whitworth, and 2/Lt.W.A.Gracey proceeded to join the 53rd Battalion Sherwood Foresters.	
			2/Lieut.W.T.J.Rumsey. took over the duties of A/Adjt from Capt.W.C.Whitworth.	
	10/4/1919		1 Other Rank proceeded to join the 52nd Battalion Sherwood Foresters.	
	13/4/1919.		Lieuts.A.J.Davis (West Yorks Regt), T.F.Carter (Sherwood Foresters), and 2/Lieut H.L.Thomson, (Leicester Regt) joined the Battalion for duty.	
	14/4/1919.		The Battalion attended a rehearsal of the PRESENTATION OF COLOURS at the No 1 Despatching Camp SANVIC.	
	16/4/1919.		ditto	
	17/4/1919.		The Battalion together with the 10th Bn Lincoln Regt rehearsed the Presentation of Colours on the parade ground No 8 Camp Harfleur, Lt Col Young.M.C. O.C.197th Inf Brigade being Present.	

Army Form C. 2118.

WAR DIARY APRIL 1919.
or
INTELLIGENCE SUMMARY.
(Erase heading not required.)

Instructions regarding War Diaries and Intelligence Summaries are contained in F. S. Regs., Part II. and the Staff Manual respectively. Title pages will be prepared in manuscript.

Place	Date	Hour	Summary of Events and Information	Remarks and references to Appendices
	18/4/1919.		The Battalion attended a rehearsal of the Presentation of the Colours before the G.O.C. 39th Division at the No 1 Despatching Camp, SANVIC. The band of the Queens Regt was in attendance.	
	22/4/1919.		Further rehearsals of the Presentation of the Colours.	
	24/4/1919.		Capt. W.E. Wright M.C. proceeded to join the 53rd Battalion Sherwood Foresters.	
	26/4/1919		Lieut. A.J. Davis assumed command of the Battalion.	

A J Davis Lieut.
Cmdg 16th Bn Sherwood Foresters.

Army Form C. 2118.

WAR DIARY
or
INTELLIGENCE SUMMARY.
(Erase heading not required.)

16 N/Derby
39

Instructions regarding War Diaries and Intelligence Summaries are contained in F. S. Regs., Part II. and the Staff Manual respectively. Title pages will be prepared in manuscript.

Place	Date	Hour	Summary of Events and Information	Remarks and references to Appendices
LE HAVRE	2/5/1919		The Battalion together with the 10th Battalion Lincoln Regt proceeded to the No 1 Dispatching Camp SANVIC to receive the King's Colours from Major General H.C.C.Uniacke C.B. C.M.G. Cmdg the Lines of Communication. The success of the ceremony was slightly marred by a bitterly cold wind, and, at the commencement, drizzling rain. Before the Colours were presented, the G.O.C. L of C gave a short address. Then came the actual presentation followed by a march past to strains of martial music discoursed by the Queens Regtl Band. Afterwards the Battalion Colour Party were photographed and then sat down to a splendid dinner in the dining hall of the No 1 Dispatching Camp. The Battalion Colour Party consisted of as follows:- Lieut.A.J.Davis (C.O.) Lieut.T.F.Carter, 2/Lieut.W.T.J.Rumsey (Officer receiving Colours) R.S.M.Arkinstall DCM, C.Q.M.S.Shaw MM Q.Q.M.S.Perkins,Cpl Barker,and Ptes Broadhead,Lovatt,Wisbey,Maidment,anscombe.	
SANVIC				
LE HAVRE	4/5/1919		The following telegram was received from 39th Division Hd Qrs. " Please convey to all ranks who took part in the Presentation of Colours, the Divisional Commanders appreciation of the excellent manner in which the ceremonial parade was carried out " The Battalion was transferred to the 117th Infantry Brigade.	
LE HAVRE	6/5/1919		Lieut.A.J.Davis handed over command of the Battalion(preparatory to demobilisation) to Lieut A.Hollett. Lieut.A.Hollett proceeded to U.K. on 15 days leave. 2/Lieut.H.L.Thomson Proceeded to U.K. for demobilisation.	
LE HAVRE	7/5/1919		Lieut.A.J.Davis and Lieut.T.F.Carter proceeded to U.K.for demobilisation. 2/Lieut.W.T.J.Rumsey assumed temporary command of the Battalion. R.S.M.Arkinstall DCM proceeded to U.K.for 1 Months furlough,at the expiration of which he is to report at the Regimental Depot,Derby.	
LE HAVRE	22/5/1919		Lieut.A.Hollett returned from 15 days leave to U.K. and assumed command of the Battalion.	

Lieut.
Cmdg 16th Battalion Sherwood Foresters.